THE SPIRIT OF THE MONTEREY COAST

THE SPIRIT OF THE MONTEREY COAST

is dedicated to my Mother

Gertrude Darkin Madison

and my Daughters

Leslie and Alison

Library of Congress Cataloging-in-Publication Data

Hobbs, Fredric.
    The Spirit of the Monterey Coast / Fredric Hobbs with contributions by Deborah Johansen.

    Includes bibliographical references and index.
ISBN 0-935382-73-9
1. Monterey Peninsula (Calif.) – History.   2. Monterey Bay Region (Calif.) – History.
I. Johansen, Deborah.   II. Title.
F868.M7H62   1990   90-11094
979.4'76 ––dc20   CIP

Printed by Spillman Printing in the United States of America

Tioga Publishing Company
P.O. Box 50490
Palo Alto, CA 94303
415-965-4081

THE SPIRIT OF THE MONTEREY COAST

FREDRIC HOBBS WITH CONTRIBUTIONS BY DEBORAH JOHANSEN AND DRAWINGS BY THE AUTHOR

TIOGA PUBLISHING COMPANY

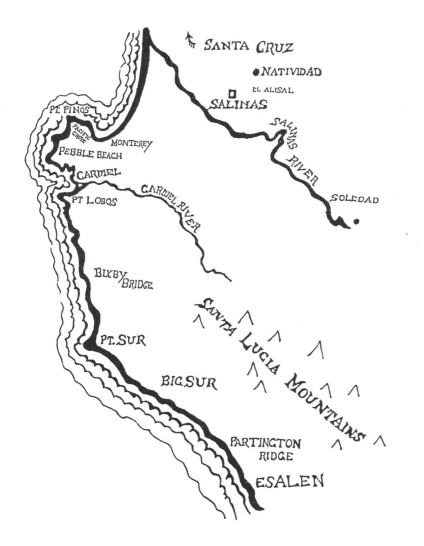

Map labels:
SANTA CRUZ
NATIVIDAD
EL ALISAL
SALINAS
PT. PINOS
PACIFIC GROVE
MONTEREY
PEBBLE BEACH
CARMEL
SALINAS RIVER
SOLEDAD
CARMEL RIVER
PT. LOBOS
BIXBY BRIDGE
SANTA LUCIA MOUNTAINS
PT. SUR
BIG SUR
PARTINGTON RIDGE
ESALEN

Table of Contents

Spirit of the Coast

*I*N CALIFORNIA, along a seventy-mile shoreline sweeping south from what has been called the barbed hook of Monterey Bay, lie coastal formations placed in another time. Sentinel rocks, worn and hollowed by the ocean, cast gentle afternoon shadows on white sand. South of Carmel, the Santa Lucia Mountains rise like mastodons at the edge of the Pacific. At Point Lobos, beyond the twisted cypress and red lichen, a promontory plunges into the surf, announcing the unrelenting wilderness that is the Big Sur country.

Green is everywhere. In the foreground, dark green softens the stark white lick of a beach. A Welsh mountainside slopes to peaceful meadows at the edge of redwoods. Iceplant glitters rose-violet through poppies. Pine boughs frame the sky, and the light fills the landscape with a glow struck from the sea. Just before sunset down the coast, the light is holy. No wonder the Benedictine Hermitage is at Santa Lucia.

The California coast from Point Lobos past the Lucias is a profound configuration of land and sea, a place of austere perfection. Artists and poets, philosophers and seers have tried to communicate its wild drama, and photographers have recorded its images. Many have remained silent before nature, for the dark green essence of the coast embodies a freedom that can overwhelm the soul.

Pilgrims have always made their way to Monterey. In early times, Native Americans were the land's only human survivors, eventually becoming unwilling servants of missionaries from a Spanish court six thousand miles away.

Under cool, low archways of adobe and tile, the fiesta life of fandangos and silver-spurred *vaqueros*, of bronze-skinned *doñas* and their colonial *dons*, echoed guitars that Sevilla never knew. The streets of old Monterey pulsed with songs of young love, bringing an era of *dolce far niente* (sweet idleness) to Spanish California.

While Puritans in the East pursued their vision of paradise through the work ethic, *los californios* found a deeper understanding of life in the bountiful valleys of Carmel and Salinas. Prior to the Gold Rush, California was an isolated "earthly paradise" unknown to New World utopians at New Harmony, Indiana, or Brook Farm, Massachusetts. On the great land-grant ranchos, the first Spanish herds flourished in the temperate climate until nearly half a million cattle roamed the grassy slopes and valleys of the Pacific frontier.

To the few outsiders who called at the port of old Monterey, the Californians were an elegant yet primitive people, uneducated and proud. They were generous to all who shared their simple human pleasures. From Sonoma south to San Diego, their hospitality was legend. The men, regarded as among the greatest horsemen of their time, were curiously disdainful of work and material reward. The women were vivacious and loving, absolute matriarchs, quite different from their Puritan sisters in New England. The human communion, the joy of alfresco *fiestas* on the beaches and in the pine forests above the sea, became a celebration of life itself. Rites of passage evolved into elaborate entertainments often lasting for three days. Rodeos introduced roping, horse racing, and bronco riding to the West.

Like the Ohlone before them, the Californians lived in harmony with the land. Their thick-walled, low, adobe buildings were early forms of organic architecture. Their diet and vigorous horsemanship kept the small population free from much of the disease prevalent in that century.

The treatment of Christianized Native Americans by missionaries was generally benign and paternal when compared with that of the slaves on southern plantations. But most labor in the fields and in the home was performed by the first Natives of California. Although the converts were not robbed of their village land by the *padres*, they were never granted full equality in the self-sufficient society of old California.

Yet in the perspective of time, old California was a warm and gentle land, where dolce far niente replaced the conquistador's lust for gold and the obsession with finding a northwest passage to India. For a brief eighty years, native sons and daughters played out their own quiet drama that formed roots of the coastal experience.

Sadly, but inevitably, families such as Vallejo, Alvarado, Figueroa, and Castro passed from view, and new generations of Yankees came to Northern California, bringing with them a new vigor and a new materialism. Yankee clipper ships now lay anchored in what Jack London called "the peacock-blue waters" of Monterey Bay. Beyond the sandy *ensenada* dust settled over cattle trails and adobe walls cracked in the last summer days of old California. Faded relics of a feudal empire were left to the ebb tides of the sea.

Mission San Carlos Borromeo collapsed over rotting timbers, leaving only the facade of a yellowing basilica to the western movement of Christianity.

To the north, rough little San Francisco was forming into a great city. A dynamic agricultural economy, directed by William Chapman Ralston and financed by gold and silver, was spawning a power-elite who gathered in the drawing rooms of grand mansions or journeyed by rail past the old Spanish thoroughfare to bask in luxury at Hotel Del Monte behind the sand dunes of Monterey. Soon laissez-faire developers talked of founding a religious colony along the pine-flecked slopes near Río del Carmelo. The Chautauqua community of Pacific Grove flourished on Point Pinos, bringing a more elegant Christianity to the land. But it was Gertrude Atherton, a novelist in search of the mythical old Monterey, who lit the beach fires that signaled the Golden Age of Carmel-by-the-Sea. Fugitives from cities rallied to a romantic vision of life on bohemian shores.

Poet George Sterling and his friend Jack London pranced on the beach and laughed at the sea. Above them, rocks echoed with the refrain of the community folk song:

> *Oh! Some folks boast of quail on toast*
> *Because they think it's tony;*
> *But I'm content to owe my rent*
> *And live on abalone.*

Mary Austin intoned free verse Amerindian laments, and beach fire entertainment gave birth to the first little theater in the West. The players drifted at the edges of the shore like jellyfish under night trees. Sterling, after composing archaic, neoclassic verses, took the cyanide pill he always kept with him.

Off the rocky coast, in the dark pacific tidepool, secrets of human existence lay buried in marine life, to become the metier of scientists and philosophers. Pioneering biologists at Hopkins Marine Station dedicated their investigations to science, while down in the saloons near Cannery Row, the eccentric philosopher Doc Ricketts talked of a new holism with his friend and collaborator John Steinbeck. On Carmel Point, the poet Robinson Jeffers, pursued the furies of the South Coast as if he were an ancient Greek.

Along 17 Mile Drive, in the greenbelt resort community founded at Pebble Beach, families of the elite sat out World War II to await the return of postwar speculators and builders who were to change the face of Monterey and Carmel forever.

Farther down the coast, artists and writers retreated from the onslaught of an increasingly mercantile society. Bridges were built by convicts chained to cliffs, and a new highway opened the way from Point Lobos to San Simeon. Up on Partington Ridge, humans shared the air and the light over Big Sur with the hawk revered by Jeffers.

Slowly, time and the green essence cooled over the redwoods. Philosophers and seers — and Henry Miller — graced the land and left it to the great mirror of the sea.

Beyond time, in the mountains near Santa Lucia, the White Hermits of Camaldoli, members of the first house of the Benedictine Order in the Western Hemisphere, live out the centuries in silence.

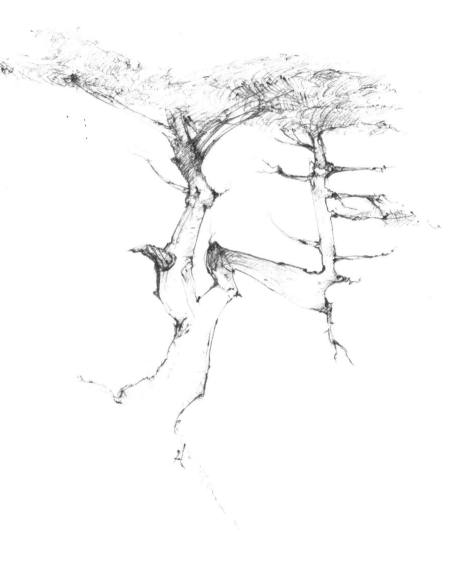

4

Footprints

Northwest Passage

When the water receded, a mountaintop appeared, and all the land that is Mònterey and beyond was covered by all oceans, and the Pacific was not yet known apart from other seas. And from the top of the mountain, the eagle, hummingbird, and coyote saw the vast waters below, and there was no trace of man nor any race of men. In the beginning, there were just the three. The eagle, who was the wisest, sent coyote down when the first bars of land appeared to see if anything remained of what was before. And coyote went, and when he returned he said to the others, "I have found one woman who will be my wife, and I sent her among the flowers to find children."

— myth of the Ohlone Tribe

IN EARLY TIMES, a soft crescent of sand rose from the waters, forming what is now called Monterey Bay. To the south, high mountains and tall trees guarded a gentle river. This was the land of Ohlone, Rumsens, and Esselens who gathered along the rich inland valleys and dark green hills of the Monterey Coast. Although their languages were distinct, the tribes shared common myths and a communion with the land. Time was measured by the yearly harvest, and survival by the rhythms of the sun and the rains.

Today, little remains of their existence. Shell mounds and hearths and a few arrowheads buried in the shifting sands are all that is left of their culture. In those days, Native Americans had no need for the golden artifacts of Empire nor for the wealth of the Indies. The land was both a touchstone for their souls and the source of their livelihood.

Along the shore, small clusters of huts nestled in the sand dunes, where the Ohlone tribelet lived lightly on the land. They did not need to venture far for food; they foraged for acorns and pine nuts or fished for sweet abalone. In the evenings, families sat together around campfires, telling stories of the mythical coyote and the hunt. Coyote, who was both a trickster and the high spirit of art, was central to the Ohlone mythology. When the Ohlone ventured into the forest to hunt, ritual prayers were intoned to Coyote, who haunted the mountains. And as each day ended, their prayers to the Great Spirit rose to the heavens with the last puff of smoke.

Deer and bear hunts were testing grounds for the Ohlone, and before a young brave went into the hills with bow and arrow, he first was summoned to his grandfather's hut, where he received the instruction to fast for three days before hiking into the wilderness. Then, once the brave reached the summit of the mountain, he invoked the spirits until he fell asleep under the night moon. When he awoke, he knew his secret dream-name. He could now hear the spirits of the air, the trees, the river, and the sea and called on them for help as he stalked the deer and the bear.

High in the mountains overlooking the villages, Coyote waited for the hunter to warn the deer of danger before vanishing again into the canyons. But the tribesman always returned to the hills, praying that the deer would consent to die before his arrow, for if the deer did not give the hunter permission to kill it, the arrow would surely miss its mark.

EVERY AGE HAS ITS DREAM, a romantic incarnation of an earthly paradise presided over by a benevolent God. So it was at the time of the discovery of the New World by the Genoese navigator Christopher Columbus. In 1542, fifty years after the discovery of the West Indies, the Catholic king of Spain ruled half the world from the Plaza Mayor in Madrid. Under the harsh light of the Iberian Peninsula, mercenary navigators and military adventurers plotted exotic crusades to the west. At the Spanish court, a vision of Marco Polo's legendary kingdom of the Indies had been implanted in the imagination of the Spanish nobility. Polo's book, a copy of which had been studied and annotated by Columbus, described voluptuous, silk-clad ebony women in a land of alabaster towers and incense. The description recalled that of the biblical City of Tarshish, "the land of gold, silver, ivory, apes, and peacocks" that enriched the Tyrean merchants and furnished the house of King Solomon. The way to this land of riches, described by both Polo and the Bible, lay in the discovery of a supposed waterway to India called the Strait of Anián.

The colony of New Spain, situated on the arid northern continent of the New World, was a far cry from Marco Polo's land of silks and elephants. By 1520, Hernando Cortés, with an army of Indians and seven hundred professional soldiers armed with muskets and cannon, and astride the first European horses on the American continent, had subdued the entire Aztec empire of Montezuma. The military victory that ended the campaign was Cortés' siege of the ancient Aztec capital of Tenochtitlán. In a battle that foretold modern tactics, thirteen Spanish brigantines, constructed on the shores of the inland lake surrounding the capital, launched a cannon-supported amphibious assault on the Aztec sacred city. The ships for this daring attack were built by Juan Rodríguez Cabrillo, a navigator-adventurer in the employ of Spain. Soon Cabrillo, at the helm of his own galleon, would sail up the coastline of what seemed to be a great island that lay beyond the territory called New Mexico.

For the next twenty years, Cortés searched for the fabled Strait of Anián and for a magical kingdom called the Seven Cities of Cibola. The grand mansions of these cities were rumored to be encrusted with gold, silver, and turquoise, and the empire was said to be ruled by a great chief. But for all his efforts, the aging *conquistador* could find no golden cities nor a waterway to the Indies. Always his dreams of riches seemed to end in an arid desert wasteland that he called "California." To both Cortés and Cabrillo, California was thought to be a mythical isle, the invention of the popular Spanish writer Ordoñez de Montalvo. It was a place of great riches, ruled by black Amazons and their queen, Califa. The island was said to be located "to the right as you sail toward the Indies."

In June 1542, Juan Rodríguez Cabrillo sailed from Navidad on the west coast of Mexico in search of the Strait of Anián. Before their ship returned home, the expedition and its crew of conscripts had charted more than one thousand miles of coastline as far north as what is now southern Oregon. This land mass became known as "Alta California" as future expeditions added details and new names to Cabrillo's pioneering achievement.

But the voyage was not a happy one. Cabrillo and his inexperienced men were swept along the coast by summer storms. Their navigational instruments were so crude that the ships were constantly off course by one or two degrees latitude.

At San Diego, which Cabrillo named San Miguel for the Archangel Michael, the first landing party waded ashore to be greeted by a group of Diequeño tribesmen. These friendly Native Americans welcomed the Spaniards and described, with sign language, the presence of the Coronado Expedition in the Southwest desert two years before. After a brief respite, Cabrillo resumed his course up the coast to discover Santa Catalina Island and Los Angeles harbor.

Following a broken northwesterly course along the Santa Barbara Channel, he pressed on, until the ships entered the choppy waters near Point Conception.

Throughout the first week of November 1542, rough seas tossed the ships through the gray rain, and, as they approached Point Pinos and the bay later known as Monterey, great ocean swells tossed the caravels off course to the west. When the northern tack was resumed a week later, the expedition sailed past the fogbound coast of Monterey Bay toward the rocky palisades of what is now Northern California. In desperation, Cabrillo, now in constant pain from a serious fall, reversed course and returned to an island sanctuary offshore. On this rocky isle, Cabrillo finally succumbed to his injuries, and his body was laid to rest by his crew and its new captain, Bartolomeo Ferrelo, who named their island refuge "Juan Rodríguez" after their brave and tenacious commander. Without further ceremony, the new captain executed Cabrillo's last command by sailing north into the winter storms.

Juan Rodríguez Cabrillo

*I*N THE SECOND HALF OF THE SIXTEENTH CENTURY, the Spanish kings shifted their focus from exploration of New Spain to development of trade with the Manila Islands in the Pacific. In 1566, the first Spanish galleon shuttled back and forth between Acapulco and Manila to exchange Montezuma's gold and silver for silks and other fine goods. Often the Manila cargo was loaded below decks in place of food for the crew on the long trek home to New Spain.

In the years that followed, the seven—month voyage to Acapulco past the stormy coast of Mendocino became a winter hell as icy winds tore away masts and scattered them like kindling wood into the sea. English pirate-explorers such as Sir Francis Drake and Thomas Cavendish descended, almost for sport, upon the slow-moving Spanish galleons to plunder them in the name of Queen Elizabeth. Small wonder that Spain grew uneasy on learning of Drake's brief landing on the West Coast at Nova Albion, above the then-undiscovered bay of San Francisco.

As the sixteenth century drew a close, a restless merchant-sea captain, Sebastián Vizcaíno, attempted to win the approval of Phillip III to survey the coast of Alta California. Surely, Vizcaíno reasoned, if he outfitted three ships at his own expense, he could discover a safe harbor near Cape Mendocino. From this land base, the returning Manila galleon would be easily provisioned and English adventurers could be prevented from plundering Spanish ships.

Vizcaíno's cool pragmatism was not lost on the king. By Royal decree, two hundred men were outfitted, under the protective eye of the Conde de Monte Rey. At Acapulco, the *San Diego*, the *Santo Tomás*, and the smaller *Tres Reyes* were prepared to make the long voyage up the coast. As final preparations were completed, three Carmelite padres arrived to join the expedition, for, in the Spanish colonial system, new frontiers were opened by both the force of arms and the force of Christianity.

At last, on May 5, 1602, with the favorable summer winds, Vizcaíno's three ships set a northwest track for Alta California, following the ghostly wake left by Cabrillo sixty years before. Six months after their festive departure from Acapulco, Vizcaíno's crew and the friars landed at the first harbor of Alta California and rechristened it San Diego, in honor of the saint's feast day. In one far-reaching proclamation, Vizcaíno formally reclaimed all lands of Alta California in the name of God and the Catholic kings of Spain. Then, after celebration of the Solemn Mass of Thanksgiving, Vizcaíno continued north along the coast to rename Santa Catalina and San Pedro islands.

As the Vizcaíno expedition sailed north past the great coastal mountain range that had been described in the logbook of Cabrillo's voyage, a curious light began to illuminate the coastline, drawing the captain's gaze closer to shore. Beyond the rocky cliffs that overhung the surf, strange, tall trees and dark pine groves cast shadows over a beautiful promontory in the late afternoon sun. Although it was December, the sea had a midsummer's calm. On December 15, 1602, with the winter sun behind him, Sebastián Vizcaíno sailed past Point Pinos to enter the blue-green waters of Monterey Bay. The next day, eighteen years before the landing of English pilgrims at Plymouth Rock, the Spanish captain and a landing party stepped ashore to claim this new land in the name of the king of Spain and his viceroy, the Conde de Monte Rey. The first mass was sung by Carmelite padres under what became known as the Vizcaíno Oak.

For three weeks, Vizcaíno foraged over the sandy terrain and through the pine forests of Point Pinos, noting in his log the spectacular physical beauty of the place he called his "noble harbor." Monterey, named for the viceroy of New Spain, seemed to Vizcaíno an earthly paradise. He noted the "infinite number of very large pines, straight and smooth, fit for masts and spars" and "oaks of prodigious size proper for building ships." He reveled in the bounty of the land, in its shellfish and wild game; and he was struck by the friendliness of the native Ohlone, who charmed him with their childlike trust.

When Vizcaíno departed Monterey, after the new year, he had completed a written report to the king of Spain:

This harbour is surrounded with rancherías of Indians, a well-looking affable people, and very ready to part with everything they have. They are also under some form of government. The arms are bows and arrows. They expressed a great deal of concern when they perceived the Spaniards were going to leave them, which happened on the 3d of Jan. 1603 when the Capitana *tender sailed out of this harbour.*

Sebastián Vizcaíno

11

DUE LARGELY TO WAR IN EUROPE, Spain lost interest in further exploration of Alta California — this time for one hundred fifty years. While Spain slept, rival nations looked covetously toward Alta California. Soon England and France would formulate a colonial policy that extended their influence to the western rim of the Pacific. From the north, Russian fur trappers continued to work the coast north of San Francisco Bay.

By 1759, the threat to Spanish dominance in the Pacific finally moved King Carlos III to action. By the mid-eighteenth century, the Spanish colonial system had developed into a complex, bureaucratic network that was an embarrassment to a new, efficiency-minded Catholic king. Letters and documents took months to pass between Madrid and Mexico City. Detailed instructions covered every contingency in the belief that the colonists would attain self-sufficiency by following a set of rules that made it unnecessary to appeal to higher authority for interpretation. Colonial policy and settlement were undertaken by a combined operation of both the military and the church — with one innovation. Carlos III disliked the independent-minded Jesuit missionaries of New Spain. So he appointed José de Gálvez inspector general to New Spain for the explicit purpose of replacing the Jesuits with a new order, the Franciscans of the Apostolic College of San Fernando.

In 1768, the viceroy of New Spain appointed a diminutive, little-known Franciscan monk, Junípero Serra, as Father Superior to this first new religious order in the New World. More than any soldier or diplomat of the times, Serra, the priest, was responsible for securing Spanish colonial dominion in Alta California.

While the bureaucrats of Mexico City and Madrid plotted to exploit their position in the New World, King Carlos III, stirred to action by the encroachment of Russian trappers on the Farallon Islands of Alta California, issued a royal decree ordering the viceroy of New Spain, the Marquis de Croix, to "guard the dominions from all invasion and insult." In October 1768, José de Gálvez and Fray Junípero Serra met in San Blas, Mexico, to discuss opening Alta California to settlement. Both men were ambitious and inspired to the task, one by a vision of earthly riches, the other by Christian zeal. Both men had risen to positions of importance through education and superior performance, and both were of humble Spanish parentage. In combination, the politician and the priest proceeded to implement Spanish policy by sheer force of will.

The following spring, at San Blas, Gálvez presented a plan for immediate occupation and colonization of San Diego and Monterey. Gálvez concurred with traditional colonial policy that colonies, once founded, must become self-sufficient so as not to burden the king's treasury, and he knew the best way to provide free labor and colonists was to convert the California natives to Christianity. Serra understood the plan well. He had been preparing for this momentous task at the Sierra Gorda mission in the high desert above Mexico City. When Gálvez unrolled his maps and documents, San Diego was marked as the first destination. Command of the expedition was assigned to the Catalan nobleman, Don Gaspar de Portolá, who had been enduring political exile as governor of Baja California's desert wasteland. Portolá welcomed his chance for glory and redemption with almost as much enthusiasm as Fray Serra, who viewed his new assignment as God's answer to his prayers.

The Mission

ON JANUARY 9, 1769, the *San Carlos*, the first of the three ships carrying Catalan volunteers, sailed up the coast to San Diego. A month later, a second vessel, the *San Antonio*, followed with two Franciscan padres. Then, after three months, the third ship, the *San José*, finally embarked laden with ten thousand pounds of dried meat, casks of good wine and brandy, twelve hundred pounds of dried figs, bushels of beans and raisins, a church bell, vestments for the friars, and other supplies essential to survival during the first year of mission life. But when the *San José* finally reached the open waters, it disappeared forever somewhere in the dark latitudes of the Pacific.

Two land parties, one under the command of Portolá and Serra, the other led by Captain Fernando Rivera, accompanied by Fray Juan Crespí, scribe of the expedition, departed north through Baja California soon after the three ships had sailed. The contingent led by Rivera and Crespí included twenty-five veterans of the frontier, forty-two Christian natives from Mission Santa María in Baja, and one hundred eighty mules. They began the three hundred-mile trek late in March. The second expedition led by Portolá and Serra left later, due to an infection in Serra's leg. Men in both parties suffered scurvy, since they carried inadequate supplies of fruits and vegetables.

The Rivera contingent completed the gruelling ordeal up the desert peninsula to Velicata mission on May 14, 1769. After pasturing the mules, they marched to San Diego in fifty-one days.

Behind them, the Portolá expedition kept up the same steady pace. Serra traveled astride a broken-down mule to save his swollen leg, as Portolá, urged on by the little priest, ruthlessly pushed his men forward to San Diego.

At the frontier outpost, the party arrived to find a makeshift camp of scurvy-ridden men who had sailed ahead on the *San Carlos* and the *San Antonio*. This grim encounter necessitated an immediate change of plans: Serra would stay in San Diego to help the survivors, while Portolá continued up the coast.

Near what is now Pismo Beach, Portolá was faced with an endless maze of quicksand and waterways that announced the inland course through the great mountains of the Coast Range. When Don Gaspar finally decided to march north past the sand dunes to the palisades above the sea, he missed the relatively flat approach to Carmel Valley.

By late October 1769, the Portolá expedition had staggered unknowingly past Monterey Bay into the giant redwood forests of the Santa Cruz Mountains. In early November, Portolá traveled farther north to the rim of the San Francisco Bay. But this bay was not the site of the earlier Vizcaíno landing. Even more disturbing, no white-sailed *San José* laden with provisions and mission bells awaited them offshore. Convinced that this body of water was not Monterey Bay, Portolá began to retrace his five hundred-mile route back to San Diego.

By December, with the party now suffering from scurvy, the expedition reached a site five miles south of Monterey harbor. During the southern march from the Santa Cruz Mountains, around Point Pinos, they saw little to corroborate Vizcaíno's glowing report of a potential port-of-call for Manila galleons. Ocean mists enveloped pine-dark promontories, and bitter winds whipped down the coast from a shoreline that seemed unprotected. The scene was a far cry from the idyllic "noble harbor" described by Vizcaíno in 1602.

Near what was in fact a great bay, Don Gaspar erected two signal crosses, one on Carmel beach and the other near Point Pinos, and began the retreat to San Diego.

Meanwhile, life in the southern outpost had deteriorated, and only the arrival of the supply ship *San Antonio* prevented abandonment of the Mission. With provisions from the ship, Portolá and Serra then readied another expedition for Monterey. The small landing party included Fray Crespí, Lieutenant Fages, and twenty soldiers and other young Spaniards who were later to become the first land-grant families of California. On Easter Sunday 1770, Serra and his party sailed for Monterey on the *San Antonio*, and Portolá and Crespí followed overland.

Springtime had imbued Portolá's men with new energy, and Serra, inspired by the arrival of the *San Antonio*, convinced them of their certain destiny to found the northernmost settlement of the Spanish Empire. When the last Portolá expedition arrived at the cross placed on Point Pinos, in late May 1769, Fray Crespí observed that it had been decorated and venerated by the local native Ohlone. Later, Serra learned that the natives had imagined that this huge cross was a sacred sign with supernatural power. To gain its favor, they had placed before it their humble offerings of friendship, love, and peace. The cross foretold the high drama of Serra's mission and his conversion of the Native Americans to a childlike understanding of Christianity.

The *San Antonio*, with Serra aboard, anchored in the bay a week after Portolá's land party had arrived. From a high vantage point near the cross at Point Pinos, positive identification of Monterey Bay was at last made. Accidentally, with almost mystical precision, the bay appeared as a perfect circle beyond the cross, an illusion that seemed to verify Vizcaíno's report to the King of Spain more than a century and a half earlier.

*J*UNÍPERO SERRA, FATHER PRESIDENT of California's missions, and Lieutenant Pedro Fages, military commander, lost no time in establishing the capital city of old California. After landing supplies from the ship, work commenced on the barracks of the Presidio of Monterey. The first buildings were hastily constructed from pine logs driven into the ground to support the mud-and-wood-reinforced walls of the enclosure. Overhead, sod roofs delineated tiny rooms that served as living quarters and a temporary chapel for the new settlers. Cannon were positioned to fire over the walls as the presidio's first line of defense. When the plaza was completed in July 1770, Don Gaspar de Portolá sailed for New Spain on the *San Antonio*, where a royal decree from a grateful king granted his retirement in Spain. Those remaining in Monterey included Lieutenant Fages, eighteen soldiers, Fray Serra, and Serra's fellow padre, Juan Crespí.

Serra's vision of a chain of missions throughout Alta California depended on the Spanish colonial model of agrarian independence. The mission was a central, strategic force within a tightly interlocking bureaucratic system that included the king, the council of the Indies, the Board of Trade, the viceroy, the military governor, the local presidio commander, and various officials of the College of San Fernando in Mexico City. The law, canon as well as civil, made no allowance for individual interpretation or independent action. Theory and practice of the law worked satisfactorily within the established tradition of the Old World. However, the padres in California interpreted the law to fit the spirit of the frontier, and most differences were settled locally, since Spanish jurisprudence moved slowly. Any successes of the administration and missionary work were to the credit of Serra's personal vision and strategy.

Junípero Serra

A year after the Presidio of Monterey was established, Serra began work on the third California mission, dedicated to San Carlos Borromeo and located on a soft, grassy slope near Carmel Bay. The Father President knew the land by Río del Carmelo would be more fertile than the sun-baked earth of the presidio compound, and, more importantly, the new site of the mission was situated near a ranchería of the Ohlone tribe.

Although a governmental order required the election of Native American officials, or local *alcaldes*, to supervise the mission *pueblo* villages, Serra strongly objected to such independence for the natives. He wanted to maintain the mission's authority over the new Christians, whom he considered politically naive and incapable of supervising themselves. However, in this matter Serra was overruled by civil authorities, and he reluctantly acceded to local elections. Yet his vow to "be wise like the serpent; simple like the dove" meant whippings for the native alcaldes if they violated the law. Serra was the supreme pragmatist when it came to pursuing "God's will."

In his private life, Serra's devotion to God was as zealous as his politics. He fasted more than was required, and the food he ate was strictly vegetarian. He interrupted his daily schedule of prayer with only a few hours of sleep. And when he was plagued with spiritual remorse, he went up to the choir loft to scourge himself, often pounding his chest with rocks. Before retiring to his cell for the night, in a further act of self-mortification, the exhausted padre would cover his bleeding body with a sackcloth robe woven together with wire that constantly scratched his open wounds. The same power that fired Serra's political expansiveness was always held in check by his equally fervent and unshakable vow of self-denial and obedience to God. Although he spoke of his inner turmoil to his close friends and his fellow padres, Crespí, Lasuén, and Palóu, the deeper struggles of the soul were confessed only to God.

The enormous task of introducing Christianity to Native Americans was crucial to Serra's lifework. The Ohlone, in particular, appealed to the Father President, and he encouraged their gentleness and curiosity in order to attract them to the mission community. Serra had an innate gift for relating to these gentle people at their own level. If they were maligned by the soldiers, he was quick to come to their defense as creatures of God. But as a disciplinarian, in defense of God's holy law, Serra was not above meting out corporal punishment, usually a severe public whipping — a fact that sullied his beatification centuries later. Before long, Serra learned rudimentary Ohlone, and his native protégés assisted him in the conversion of the tribal families. Lessons were held for the baptized natives, who intoned prayers and songs in the mission courtyard. To further encourage Christianization, Serra exchanged gifts of brightly colored cloth and beads for offerings of seeds and nuts from the rancherías. Although he ran the mission with a firm hand, the little priest instilled a trust that made the Carmel mission a model for others along the coast. It was Serra's personal inspiration that saved Mission San Carlos from the violence that erupted later at San Diego and San Gabriel.

During the first years, inadequate food supplies discouraged the natives from accepting the Christian community. But with the arrival of the *Santiago* in May 1772, the situation improved. The ship brought supplies that meant survival for the settlement. In addition, the first Mexican women to arrive on the Monterey Coast were on board. This finally convinced the natives that the padres were not the offspring of their mules, but were born of women, just as they were.

As the mission community flourished and the number of baptisms increased, Serra's treatment of the natives as creatures of God was often at odds with his strict denial of their civil rights.

*A*T MONTEREY AND RÍO DEL CARMELO, Serra's vows of obedience finally led to an inevitable confrontation between the religious and civil authorities who ruled the settlement. Serra was not above calling Governor Pedro Fages to task, and the ambitious career officer considered the demanding padre a constant irritant. Increasingly disgruntled with his assignment in primitive Alta California, the high-born Fages was mystified by Serra's genuine enthusiasm for mission life on the frontier. Unfortunately, the few miles of heavy forest that separated church and state on the Monterey Peninsula did little to buffer the two indomitable personalities, who often disagreed over such matters as soldiers' conduct, food rations, and treatment of the Native Americans.

In time, Serra appealed to higher authorities to clarify the respective roles of the military and the mission in colonization and to set forth a plan for the missionary effort in California. In one of the most critical decisions of his career, Serra decided to attempt the long journey to Mexico City to present his petition to the Father Superior at the College of San Fernando. Not to be outdone, Fages sent a letter in his own defense to the new viceroy, Antonio María Bucareli y Ursua.

Once in Mexico City, Serra was granted a personal audience with Bucareli, who was immediately won over by the intelligence and forceful personality of the Father President. Together they agreed upon a grand strategy for mission policy throughout California. Serra's document known as the *Reputación*, was a masterpiece of visionary enlightenment and political expediency that would further the cause of Christianity in the New World. In his personal dealings with Bucareli, Serra proved a master negotiator, proposing maritime strategy and more effective overland supply routes within the mission system. He also succeeded in obtaining greater civil rights for the missionaries, privacy of missionary mail, standardization of weights and measures, improved food rations, and control over missionary assignments and the breeding of cattle. Through the unprecedented efforts of Serra, the missions would also gain control over education and administration of the Christianized natives. The military was clearly placed in the secondary position of preserving the peace. As a final political and personal victory for Serra, the unhappy Fages was replaced by Fernando de Rivera y Moncada.

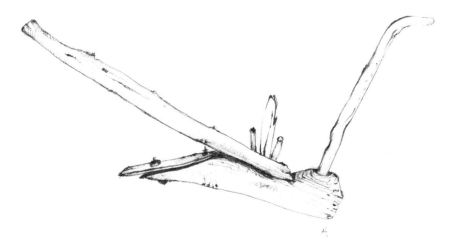

At Mission San Carlos, the Father President returned to the strenuous life of political struggle and Christianization of Native American neophytes.

In the ensuing years, as he approached his seventh decade, Serra's frail constitution weakened further. In the midst of the founding of Mission Dolores near San Francisco Bay, the bureaucratic problems with the military commander escalated. The founding of his ninth mission at Santa Barbara, on Easter Day 1782, was the Father President's last mission. His beloved Crespí had died two years earlier. The threat that the Dominican Order would replace the Franciscans as missionaries in California only added to Serra's discouragement.

At dawn on August 28, 1784, Serra suffered acute chest pains. Seated in meditation on a little stool in the bare adobe cell, Serra requested Palóu to sprinkle holy water around the room. Comforted by the company of his friend, Serra accepted a cup of broth at midday and then lay wearily on his wooden bed for a short siesta. When Palóu returned, he found his Father President and friend peacefully at rest forever.

Serra's spirit would be felt for years to come by those who followed his footsteps. In 1797, Fray Francisco de Lasuén completed the most beautiful of California's missions. Restored in the 1930s by Sir Harry Downie, San Carlos Borromeo stands *in memoriam* to the opening of the Pacific frontier.

Mission San Carlos Borromeo

Dolce far Niente

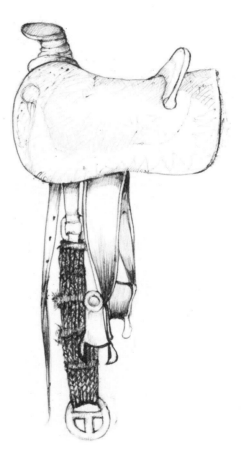

PLYMOUTH ROCK and the Charter Oak heralded the advent of puritanical English colonial society on the Atlantic Coast. In Alta California, Monterey spawned a unique Mediterranean culture along the Pacific frontier. Great Native American nations and the rugged Continental Divide stood as a barrier to these two diverse and influential social orders. The path west was tortuous and far more time-consuming than the journey to the New World. As a consequence, California remained isolated from the East during the American Revolution. And the Monterey Coast eventually transcended its early beginnings as a primitive missionary settlement to become the birthplace of a new western spirit, where leisure and good-hearted hospitality contrasted with the bleak austerity of New England.

Although the people of Monterey knew little of the American Revolution and the surrender of the British at Yorktown, the power-elite in Madrid and Mexico City had not lost sight of the Californians in their scheme for geopolitical control of Alta California. Antonio Bucareli, Mexico's most intelligent and competent viceroy, had pushed forward the colonization of Alta California with his best military commanders and the visionary priest Junípero Serra. There, settlements soon forced England and Russia to consolidate their outposts closer to their highly profitable fur trading enterprise in Canada and Alaska.

By 1775, Spain had decreed Monterey capital of California. And after the founding of several new missions, including Mission Dolores at San Francisco, the colonial population slowly advanced from 600 to 3,270 within two generations.

The golden pastoral age of Monterey had begun under the aegis of Father President Serra and his Franciscan missionaries. These Spanish intellectuals, who were highly educated ascetics and master teachers of Christianity, also became farmers, traders, cattlemen, bankers, and innkeepers — skills necessary to carry out the Spanish colonial doctrine of self-sufficiency in California. Their consecrated lodgings were always given without price to horsemen traveling up the coast to Yerba Buena and south to San Diego.

Thus began the tradition of joyful, warmhearted fellowship on the adobe verandas of old California — a life-style known as dolce far niente (sweet idleness). Elegant and gracious evenings became events of human communion between visitor and host. As word of California hospitality spread to the outside world, Monterey became a picturesque port of call for voyagers to the Pacific. During the legendary pastoral period of 1781 to 1841, the inhabitants of old Monterey intuitively knew they were custodians of a truly timeless land.

In the beginning, life was hard. Men performed basic tasks of family and garrison work; women occupied themselves with housekeeping or supervised native servants at domestic chores and child care. Each morning, dressed in black, the ladies of old Monterey attended mass in the presidio and then retired to a day of domesticity. On a balmy afternoon the Californians might picnic outside the settlement walls by the bay. Beyond the adobe presidio, community gardens and pastures, and deep pine forests beckoned like a child's dream of paradise.

The principal entertainment in the very early days of Monterey included dancing, singing, and card playing. The Spanish tradition of fiesta by torchlight held forth in forest glens and coves, where pine-pitch fires illuminated a dance floor, and the salt air was steeped with the pungency of burning resin from the torches. On Sunday nights, the governor extended the hospitality of his personal quarters, as violins and guitars played out the romantic songs of Castile and Sevilla six thousand miles away.

In the years after Serra's death, a new generation married young and delighted their families with a dozen or more offspring. Horses roamed the territory, and it was said that a true Californian was born in the saddle, for in the later years of the ranchos, infants were taken at birth, on horseback, to the closest mission for baptism by the padres. With herds of cattle and Andalusian horses flourishing in the rich valleys from Santa Barbara to the Carmel mission, horsemanship and a unique concern with the outdoors became the mark of the Californians. In the ritual of California hospitality, a visitor was presented with a gift horse after his stay in old Monterey.

The most spectacular fiesta of old California was the rodeo, with its vaqueros resplendent in yellow and silver, and the roundup of horses for branding. Often the event was combined with Monterey's version of the bullfight, in which horse racing and bronco riding preceded the deadly combat of grizzly bears and bulls. By the turn of the nineteenth century, the California vaqueros ranked with the most skilled and sophisticated horsemen in the world. Their ornate dress, stamped leather and silver saddles, and skills with a lariat were legendary.

The inauguration of a governor or the visit of a dignitary were occasions for the mannered theatricality of the provincial capital. Crowded inside some fifty presidio buildings — in primitive living conditions — the Californians always welcomed the opportunity to perform. Equestrian entertainments and bear-and-bull battles were staged with such flair and joie de vivre that visitors such as Commodore George Vancouver and Richard Henry Dana were intrigued by the storybook capital and its Spanish-speaking people. In *Two Years Before the Mast*, Dana noted that

> *every rich man looks like a grandee and every poor scamp like a broken-down gentleman. I have often seen a man with a fine figure and courteous manners, dressed in broadcloth and velvet, with a noble horse completely covered with trappings: without a* real *in his pockets and absolutely suffering for something to eat.*

The land of dolce far niente had established a social order and life-style in a Mediterranean tradition that was uniquely Californian. A large and proud family was the respected foundation of society. Children venerated their fathers and mothers. Boys grew into strapping outdoorsmen, who lived healthy lives under the California sun without the benefit of trained doctors. The women, vivacious and full of life, possessed a beauty quite apart from their puritan sisters in the East. The Californians never seemed to suffer for lack of formal education; their elegant manners and many of their customs were passed down by the founding families of Monterey.

Gradually, as the agrarian mission economy became more productive, the community began to look beyond the presidio to a life on the rancho. Later, when local garrison soldiers retired from service, they were rewarded with generous land grants in the fertile, rolling valleys surrounding Monterey. Most of the grants did not transfer ownership of major acreage to the *hijos del país* (native sons) until the Mexican period. But following the lead of the retired pioneer corporal, Manuel Boranda, other settlers built adobes outside the Presidio on the mesa overlooking Monterey Bay.

The romance lasted eighty years, from the early days of Serra's founding of the Carmel mission to the American occupation. Time passed slowly on this sunlit land by the Pacific. Picnics became elaborate social events, *meriendas* under a lazy turquoise sky. Young lovers revived the Spanish tradition of breaking lavender-scented eggshells on each other's heads. And the sight of a dark-haired señorita riding home before her yellow-coated vaquero along the coastline at sunset conjured up a vision of the romantic sublime that was the essence of old Monterey. In the cool evenings, adobe courtyards echoed with songs of California, accompanied by Spanish guitars.

During this century of struggle, imperialism, and frontier hardship, the men and women of Monterey stepped back from time, asking for nothing but love from their families and peace with their neighbors, offering the hand of friendship to strangers who passed their way. It is one of history's few pleasant ironies that the descendants of the conquistadores who came to the New World searching for riches found instead a life of higher value on the land of California.

Los Californios
and the Americans

DURING THE FINAL DECADES of dolce far niente, the outside world cast its exploitive eye on the Monterey Coast. With the exception of Brazil, Spain had ruled South America and a central continent that had included what is now Texas, New Mexico, Arizona, and California for almost three centuries. But with the overthrow of King Ferdinand VII by Napoleon, in 1808, a spirit of revolution and independence seized the New World.

Since the conservative mission padres were loyal to Spain, California remained apart from the movement sweeping South America. Yet to the insurgent anti-imperialist Spanish colonies, the isolated position of the Californians invited attack. In 1818, an expedition under the command of the French pirate Hippolyte de Bouchard was commissioned by the revolutionary government of Buenos Aires to capture the poorly defended capital at Monterey.

As Bouchard and three hundred and sixty—six patriots and freebooters outfitted their ships at a forward base in Hawaii, the American clipper *Clarion* raced to Monterey with warning of an impending attack by sea. At Monterey, Governor Pablo Vicente de Sola nervously stirred the usually placid Californians to action. Women and children were evacuated to the Salinas Valley and to Mission Soledad. A second line of defense was established at Monterey behind twenty-four cavalrymen and eleven artillerymen with three cannon. The entire garrison numbered less than a hundred men, including vaqueros with lariats and Native Americans armed with bows and arrows.

Although ammunition for eight rusty field guns was in limited supply, the motley force met the demands for surrender with a vow to fight to the last man. Bouchard's ship and the men on shore exchanged a harmless round of fire. After a brief skirmish near Point Pinos, Sola regrouped and reinforced his small army from garrisons in San Francisco. The Californians retreated to the Salinas Valley. During that time, Bouchard's invaders slaughtered stray cattle, looted the presidio, and set fire to the thatched rooftops of adobe homes before they withdrew.

Sola and his combined forces returned to the sight of a burned-out capital. Except for the church, all buildings had been torched or vandalized. Stores of soap, tallow, lard, and food had been deliberately ruined. Reconstruction began immediately, but months went by before families could be reunited in their newly rebuilt adobes. For the next three and one-half years, the pastoral tempo and rhythm of life returned to the land, as Monterey refused to join the independence movement.

IN APRIL 1822, Monterey's Governor Sola, emboldened by the success of Napoleon against Spain, proclaimed that Mexico had declared independence from the court of Madrid. The crowd at the Presidio repeated an oath of allegiance to a new and less distant master. The ancient cannon that had last fired against Bouchard boomed out a salute that echoed across Monterey Bay.

By now, the outside world had assessed Monterey. Comte de La Pérouse, the French marine scientist; George Vancouver, the British naval explorer; trappers and others from Russia and the United States — all had cast a civilized eye on the isolated coastal town. Many young men saw a fortune beyond the shoreline of Point Pinos. Some jumped ship to join the new generation of Californians. Others came to trade and to merge their resources and bloodlines with Monterey's founding families.

William Hartnell of Lancashire, England, was the first young Anglo to find love and fortune in Monterey. He organized a trading company that proposed to exploit new land grant ranchos near the Salinas River. For awhile, the Californians ignored the new commerce as an unnecessary interruption of their carefree life, but as Mexico opened Monterey and San Diego to international shipping, Yankee clipper ships and cargo vessels from England and France docked at these new deep-water ports.

The character of Monterey began to change, population increased, and walled adobes began to cover the mesa. Horse paths and oxen trails were widened into roads, and rude plank bridges were built over eroded gullies along the Calle Principal.

Now a successful partner in his trading firm, Hartnell eventually married the beautiful señorita Teresa de la Guerra. Through such marriages, Anglo-American blood became mixed with the blood of such founding land grant families as the Soberanes, the Castros, and the Vallejos.

THE ENDLESS DAYS of good-hearted life on the valley ranchos and in the town were upset, in the 1830s, by active Californian resistance to high-handed Mexican politicians who taxed the California seaports. At the same time, secularization and spoilage of the beautiful mission network formally ended the dominion of the church in Alta California.

In 1833, a new governor, General José Figueroa, initiated three years of peace by granting large ranchos to Monterey families. Even Cristina Delgado, a widowed Carmel mission Native American, received rich lands at the mouth of the Salinas River. Other Anglo-Americans received grants as a result of intermarriage; and in 1834, Figueroa officially divided the huge Rancho El Alisal between the Soberanes and Hartnell, upon whose land was founded a boarding school.

As these properties were transferred, Thomas O. Larkin, half-brother of American merchant Juan Bautista Cooper, arrived in Monterey from Massachusetts by way of Yerba Buena.

Thomas O. Larkin

WITH TYPICAL YANKEE VIGOR, Thomas O. Larkin embarked on a plan to exploit the supposed naiveté of the Californians. After all, Larkin reasoned, the simple Mediterranean society traded hides for silk and satin that their doñas wore at galas inside crude earthen-floored adobes. To take fair business advantage of such an impractical people seemed an easy matter.

It was not common knowledge that the foreign trade monopoly was in the hands of Hartnell and a group of Yankees who had married into the major pioneer land grant families. Larkin, equally shrewd, resolved to capture a piece of the hide and tallow business for himself. He joined forces with his half-brother, Juan Bautista Cooper, from whom he borrowed five hundred dollars to establish a trading and import store near the Custom House. At first, business was less than brisk. But soon Larkin was busy ordering fancy dresses and other more flamboyant goods from such new sources of materials and credit as Mexico and Hawaii. Since the word of a Californian was considered sacred, it was thought to be improper to press the dons for payment and many accounts remained delinquent for years. Larkin, with Cooper's help, quietly acquired these accounts in order to set up a clearing house for the considerable debts of the first families. When at last the hides were collected from rancheros to pay off the drafts, Larkin charged a considerable service fee. Eventually, his store and clearing house acquired the status of a small bank. Nor did the resourceful Yankee stop with this opportunistic venture. He proceeded to bribe revenue officials to devalue the outrageous tariffs imposed by the Mexican government. Although this procedure was not new to Monterey, Larkin continued to flaunt the traditions of old California for his own profit.

Among all the Yankees, only Larkin chose not to marry into a California family. In the fall of 1833, he married the light-haired, fair-skinned Rachel Holmes, recent widow of a Honolulu resident, at a shipboard ceremony off the coast of Santa Barbara. After a rousing fiesta onshore, the couple set up housekeeping in a large, new home overlooking Monterey Bay. The new residence quickly became the gossip of the town. The house was the first two-story example of "Monterey Colonial" architecture that combined Spanish adobe style and indigenous building materials with traditional New England design.

The construction of the Larkin house symbolized the force of change that would overcome the tranquility and isolation of pastoral California. Before the introduction of external commerce, the Californians had been custodians of a frontier land. Now, many Americans, finding a better life in California, retired from commerce and shopkeeping to become masters of huge land-grant ranchos and barons of vast herds of cattle that roamed the rich countryside.

These new mixed-blood generations altered the course of history forever. More ships entered Monterey Bay to transport the burgeoning hide-and-tallow trade to Honolulu and Boston. And the outside world was beginning to know the true worth of California. Soon the produce of its soil, its underground mineral wealth, and ultimately the land itself, would become the commodity of even more ambitious entrepreneurs.

*I*N THE WET SPRING OF 1834, Governor José Figueroa, known as "El Pacífico," received final orders from Mexico City to secularize the missions. Accompanying this directive was a document granting Figueroa the retirement he had long requested. According to the document, his replacement, José María Híjar, would be accompanied by a group of exiled radicals, together with two hundred fifty new colonists. El Pacífico calculated, perhaps correctly, that this influx of Mexicans might well trigger chaos in the orderly and peaceful capital province. Thus, the governor wisely elected to modify and delay secularization by means of gradual phasing out of the missions over a two-year period. Half the mission lands were to be returned to the Christian Native Americans; the remaining property was to be administered by the civilian government in the old Spanish colonial tradition.

This orderly transfer of power was suddenly disrupted by political upheaval in Mexico City. Upon arrival in Monterey, Híjar, El Pacífico's replacement discovered that he, in turn, had been replaced by a Mexican army colonel, Mariano Chico.

But Juan Bautista Alvarado, and Mariano Vallejo, young liberal friends of El Pacífico, did not wish to surrender secularized mission properties to a new Mexican administrator — now that large land grants were at stake.

Without hesitation, the emerging liberal leaders of the hijos del país convened the provincial government in Monterey and immediately voted to retain the sick and aging El Pacífico. The old governor then summarily deported the radical contingent to Mexico.

In the final year of his administration, Figueroa granted no less than eight additional tracts of land in Monterey, Carmel Valley, and across the river from Mission Soledad, to influential pioneer Californians. Then, in late September 1835, El Pacífico died of apoplexy, an event that heralded trouble and political unrest in the capital province.

Colonel Mariano Chico's administration was a disaster for Monterey. The fact that he lived with a young mistress deeply offended the family-oriented doñas of Monterey. And soon after he became involved in a vendetta against the merchants' trade monopoly, Chico retreated to Mexico City.

Juan Bautista Alvarado and his young hijos then reinstalled their members into the *disputación*, where their assembly president, José Castro, immediately proclaimed the sovereignty of California and made its native son Alvarado governor. In the celebration that followed, the halcyon days of dolce far niente came alive again on the Monterey Coast.

Yankees and Spanish Californians danced from twilight to dawn. As brandy inspired the throng in an ecstasy of sensuality and nostalgia for their land, the men moved like noble princes with their elegantly clothed señoritas to stately rhythms of the *contradanza*, the wild, swirling *fandango*, and the leaping *jota*. Thus, the new year 1837 was christened in a glow of pine-pitch torches and the music of guitars and violins.

The new governor, a popular hijo del país, was not the golden hero his supporters had envisioned. By his thirtieth birthday, Alvarado's administration had led Monterey once more to the point of chaos and near anarchy. The instability of Alvarado's personal life inevitably affected the political environment. His drinking became chronic, his body was fat, and his countenance reflected the ravages of late nights and too much brandy. He left his beautiful mistress, Raimunda Castillo, who had born him three children out of wedlock, for a marriage of political alliance. Even on his wedding day, he insulted his bride, the sensitive young Martina Castro, whom he had never seen, by sending his half-brother José Estrada to stand in for him at the ceremony. The governor was detained by "official business" —

though it was reported that Juan Bautista had been detained by a rendezvous with a bottle for several nights before the nuptials.

By the early 1840s, more foreigners had established themselves in the port of Monterey. One fact was now inescapable: The influx of *los Yanquis* could not be stopped. The first party of immigrants from the eastern United States was already on its way west across the Great Plains to the Pacific frontier.

Juan Bautista Alvarado soon paid the price for the support of one such newcomer, Isaac Graham, a distillery operator and freebooter from nearby Natividad, who had lent troops to Alvarado. Graham, drunk on the streets of Monterey and accompanied by his cohorts with their Tennessee long rifles, frequently insulted the new governor, drunkenly shouting for the overthrow of California and constantly threatening the governor's life. Finally, a priest warned the governor of Graham's plot to capture Monterey by force. It was now imperative that Alvarado move against Graham.

Alvarado could neither hide from his former ally nor tolerate Graham's challenge. One early morning, Alvarado gathered a band of hijos del país to capture Graham at his distillery-saloon in Natividad. The resulting arrests were quickly followed by the deportation of Graham, along with anyone of Spanish descent not married to a native daughter. These prisoners of war were taken to a jail in Mexico City, where the government charged Graham's "army" with insurrection. Then, back in Monterey, the governor turned to a more immediate problem: the takeover of land by the Yankees.

Juan Bautista Alvarado

At the same time, Thomas Larkin was rumored to be actively working toward annexation by the United States and publicly appeared in the Eastern press, extolling the virtues of homesteading in California. Such advertising brought the Bidwell-Bartleson party west in classic American pioneer fashion.

From his estate-garrison in Sonoma on the northern frontier, General Mariano Vallejo demanded support from Mexico to hold the interior outposts against foreign incursions. While Mexico City deliberated, and Larkin lobbied for annexation, a distracted and increasingly morose Juan Bautista Alvarado looked to his friends for comfort and relief from the toils of administration. At the beginning of 1841, Alvarado purchased Rancho El Alisal from his friend Feliciano Soberanes and moved his family permanently out of the capital city into the valley. His fellow hijos del país benefitted from their past loyalty, as Juan Bautista embarked on the largest and most generous program of land grants in the short history of California.

His friends, his family, and even his former mistress received free land grants that put the bulk of fertile land surrounding Monterey in the hands of a few old California families.

In the final two years of his administration, Alvarado awarded twenty-eight land-grant ranchos, totaling almost three hundred thousand acres, in Salinas and Carmel valleys and at Mission Soledad. Nor did the governor forget the presidio soldiers. In what was the last investment by a nearly bankrupt administration, he completed El Cuartel, the officers' barracks, the most elaborate city building of the time in old Monterey.

Old Monterey, 1842

*I*N AUGUST 1842, the territory's last governor, General Manuel Micheltorena, accompanied by three hundred irregular troops arrived in Los Angeles. But to the amazement of the Monterey colony, Micheltorena was to remain in Southern California with his army — ostensibly for his health — for more than two years. As a consequence of his eccentric and cowardly behavior, the new governor missed the strange events of October 19 and 20, 1842, at Monterey harbor.

During the afternoon siesta hours of October 19, Thomas Larkin and a small group of people, who happened to be awake, looked down at the harbor to behold two armed American ships, the sloop *United States* and the frigate *Cyane*. A third vessel, *Joven Guipúzcoana*, which had departed Monterey earlier in the day, appeared to be a prisoner of the American warships. A crisis of fear seized the town as people awakened from their siestas to find themselves at the mercy of the United States Squadron in the Pacific under the command of Commodore Thomas Catesby Jones. Defense of the port by an ill-equipped police force of twenty-nine garrison soldiers was unthinkable. When Commodore Jones sent surrender demands to the governor of Alta California, Alvarado forwarded the document, like unwanted mail, to the commandant of the presidio guard. On receipt of the demand, the old commandant arranged for a formal surrender ceremony the next morning, in spite of Larkin's efforts to convince Commodore Jones that no state of war yet existed between the United States and Mexico.

On October 22, one hundred fifty American marines, sailors, and bandsmen marched down Calle Principal to the entrance of El Cuartel, where the American commodore formally took possession of the Mexican capital of Alta California. Then, as the Stars and Stripes ran up the flagpole, a deafening salute rang out across Monterey Bay. By late afternoon, the town was in a state of mass hysteria as both Larkin and Hartnell calmly argued with the American commander. The verbal battle continued well into the evening. Jones held to his rationale of preventing the British from capturing Monterey, and Larkin produced written communications from both American and Mexican officials that proved no war existed between the two countries.

Less than twenty-four hours after the United States flag was raised over the city, the Mexican flag replaced the American colors. The commodore, at last convinced by Larkin, had restored Monterey to Mexico. On board the American flagship, Jones held a party for visiting Californians, and after the town had reciprocated the American hospitality with a formal fiesta on land, the warships sailed out of Monterey Bay.

By summer 1844, the citizens of Monterey were still savoring the last days of dolce far niente. The Custom House had been renovated for the entertainment of visiting naval officers and Thomas Larkin and his new wife now celebrated the Fourth of July with the founding families in their new two-story home overlooking the harbor.

At Rancho El Alisal, under the shade of great oaks, Juan Bautista Alvarado talked politics with his old friend José Castro, now military commandant of the northern province. Their retreat to the ranchos had been a happy withdrawal. But their capital city, a town of some three hundred buildings, was fast becoming a seaport of merchants and foreign sailors, who too often returned the flirtatious smiles of young señoritas. Larkin was still secretly pushing for annexation by America. In Los Angeles, Governor Micheltorena was doing nothing to contain his *cholo* (half-breed) army of rapists and thieves. At home, Micheltorena's grant to Alvarado of the 44,360-acre Rancho las Mariposas in the Sierra foothills had done little to quiet the ex-governor's concern for tranquility of the province.

Alvarado Adobe

In the courtyard of José Castro's large adobe near Mission San Juan Bautista, a force of two hundred twenty men, recruited from the northern frontier, gathered under Alvarado's charismatic leadership. Word had spread throughout California that the Swiss-German trader John Sutter was training a Native American army at his fort in Sacramento, for the purpose of taking control of California. This act of political treachery especially outraged Alvarado, for it was he who had granted this land in the north to Sutter, five years before, when the trader was penniless in Monterey. As a final insult, Sutter's sympathizers were rumored to be joining Micheltorena's army in Los Angeles. The specter of civil war loomed like a Goyaesque presence on the land, as the patriotism of Alvarado's oratory stirred his fellow rancheros to action.

The first point of contact between the insurgent hijos del país and Micheltorena's irregulars was at San José, where half of the cholo army was routed in a brief encounter that forced Micheltorena's retreat to the south. This time, the cholos refused to abandon the territory so easily. Soon Juan Bautista Alvarado, accompanied by his old comrades Pío Pico and José Castro, rode into the valley toward Los Angeles, leading four hundred vaqueros recruited from ranchos throughout California. The battle, a running two-day skirmish in the San Fernando Valley, was a confused, violent choreography of men and horses, with no apparent casualties other than the animals. Much gunpowder was expended without hitting the target, and by the end of the second day, a pall of blue-gray mist hung over the two exhausted armies like a cloud on the landscape.

In the brief two days of fighting, Mexico's stranglehold on Alta California was broken. Pío Pico assumed the new governorship and proclaimed Los Angeles the capital, a pragmatic decision based on the knowledge that he had little influence beyond Santa Barbara. José Castro and his entourage assumed control of the treasury at the Monterey Custom House, while his friend, Juan Bautista retired again to the good life at Rancho El Alisal. To the north, General Mariano Vallejo, the most refined and educated figure in old California, watched nervously from a neutral position at his baronial rancho in Sonoma. As for Micheltorena, he rode at the head of his cholos to Monterey, where he sailed in relative comfort to his home in Mexico. California was now divided into a group of primitive city-states, separated not only by terrain but by the personalities of the hijos del país.

Captain John Charles Fremont

34

Prelude to Annexation

IN 1845, CHANGES OCCURRED that resulted in the eventual annexation of Alta California by the United States of America. In the spring of the year, Secretary of State James Buchanan, with the support of President James K. Polk, offered the Mexican government a paltry forty million dollars for Alta California and New Mexico. Then while "scientific" expeditions were being prepared by the army for the stated purpose of surveying the Far West, a secret diplomatic pouch was relayed to the newly appointed United States consul for California. The man who received this message was none other than the respected Monterey businessman Thomas O. Larkin.

Always the pragmatist, Larkin had mastered the subtle art of politics. Still secretly nurturing his desire for the nonviolent takeover of California by the United States, the consul had great confidence in the success of the annexation plan, until a United States warship brought conflicting reports to San Francisco that war would soon be declared against Mexico.

Events seemed to be overtaking the citizens of Monterey. In the north, General Mariano Guadalupe Vallejo, protector of the frontier and longtime advocate of law and order, was rumored to sympathize with the cause of annexation. Outside Monterey, José Castro, commander of the province, was busy moving his munitions and military establishment to Rancho El Alisal, where he intended to headquarter his defense of California. This action did not go unnoticed by the Californians, who proceeded about their business with increasing anxiety and suspicion of all.

Such was the atmosphere of old Monterey as its citizens prepared Christmas *piñatas* for the celebration of *La Noche Buena* and the fiestas to follow during December 1845. A week before Christmas, their world of isolation and gaiety collapsed with the arrival of heavily armed horse soldiers commanded by Captain John Charles Fremont of the United States Engineers. After camping and reprovisioning his men at Sutter's Fort, in the Sacramento Valley, Fremont rode out unaccompanied on a mission to meet with Larkin, the American consul, and José Castro, the military commandant. Castro, who believed that Fremont's troops were a surveying mission of armed civilians, politely granted the dashing American officer permission to bivouac at nearby Rancho Laguna, on the condition that he would not molest the settlement. But Fremont was a devious and ambitious officer, and his word to the commander of Monterey — in spite of Larkin's assurances — was, at best, suspect. It was no surprise to the Californians that, in March 1846, Fremont arrived in force at the rancho of William Hartnell.

Fremont had no sooner set up camp with armed cavalry than Castro threatened to expel the Yankees from California. The cause for Castro's action was understandable: A small group of Fremont's men had stopped at the neighboring home of Castro's uncle and had treated the old renchero's daughter rudely. The American commander was the son-in-law of Senator Thomas

Hart Benton, and a man given to grandiose visions of himself as emperor of the West. He reacted in anger at the manner in which Castro's messenger had presented him with the ultimatum, and after vowing to fight to the last man, Fremont retreated only as far as the foothills of Gabilan Peak, where with great flourish, he raised the American flag over the Salinas Valley and dared the Californians to take down the colors in battle.

But the showdown between Castro and Fremont did not take place. Before Castro could organize a mounted army large enough to dislodge the haughty American, Fremont withdrew to pursue a romantic, headline-making exploration of Oregon. His departure was greeted with the announcement of Alcalde Díaz that "all is now tranquil in Monterey."

*I*N JUNE 1846, an uprising of American settlers, known as the Bear Flag Revolt, and President James Polk's declaration of war against Mexico over a minor Texas border incident only increased the probability of an American takeover. In Monterey, the streets were full of silent, sullen-looking Californians. Rumors of the arrival of *gringo* squatters swept through Monterey like the wind off Point Pinos. It seemed a certainty that the ruthless and hot-tempered Fremont would return to burn their homes, rape their women, and steal their land. Larkin's carefully laid plan for peaceful annexation was greeted with despondent sighs by any leader still willing to listen to the American consul.

Only Don Mariano Vallejo argued persuasively and intelligently for the annexation of California by the United States. Yet when he proceeded to instruct his fellow hijos del país in the checks and balances of the American constitutional system, he was received by shouts for California freedom and independence. Larkin, who was now strangely quiet, had been secretly instructed by Secretary of State Buchanan to urge California leaders toward statehood by first declaring themselves a republic, free from Mexico. He did not have long to wait.

On June 8, 1846, William B. Ide, a former Vermont schoolmaster, set forth an overblown manifesto declaring his Sonoma settlement an independent republic. His flag, painted on cotton and decorated with pieces of a red flannel miner's shirt, included a lone star and a grizzly bear. The stated revolutionary goal of the "Bear Flaggers" was the establishment of a government that would respect the rights of United States settlements in California.

José Castro immediately dispatched a fifty-man police force to put down the rebellion, but the brave Californians were no match for the superior numbers of veteran frontiersmen. In a violent, running battle, the Monterey horsemen suffered severe casualties. Only clever defensive tactics and knowledge of the terrain saved them from complete annihilation at the hands of a pursuing force that now included Fremont and his horsemen, who had returned from the Oregon border.

The "Bear Flaggers" soon became part of the annexation of California by American force of arms.

A T THE MONTEREY CUSTOM HOUSE, acting on advance information from Washington, Consul Larkin looked forward to an unusually dramatic celebration on the Fourth of July 1846. Once again the consul was to see his plans for peaceful takeover ruined by the hard reality of combat. During the spring months, the United States Pacific Squadron, under the command flag of Commodore John D. Sloat, waited cautiously at Mazatlán, on the west coast of Mexico, for a formal declaration of war by the United States before executing standing orders to seize all California ports. When the commodore received news that the hostilities had broken out along the Río Grande River in Texas, Sloat dispatched the *Cyane*, the *Levant*, and the *Savannah* to Monterey. And on July 2, two days before his usual Fourth of July gala, Thomas O. Larkin looked out his window to see the American fleet at anchor in Monterey harbor.

Four days of unbearable tension followed, while Sloat, not wanting to repeat Jones' blunder of 1842, deliberated on his orders to seize the port. The old commodore feared that if he delayed any longer, the British fleet that had been sighted off the coast of Baja California, or vaquero militia from the ranchos might arrive to interfere with his landing. For one last time, Consul Larkin pleaded for patience, still certain that the Californians would abdicate peacefully. Finally, on July 6, after digesting the news of the Bear Flag Revolt — now led by Fremont — Sloat incorrectly concluded that the seemingly impulsive Fremont must be acting under orders from Washington.

Old Monterey Custom House

THE NEXT MORNING at seven o'clock, Sloat sent Commandante Castro his terms of surrender. By ten o'clock, his disciplined, "spit-and-polish" corps of marines marched unopposed to the Monterey Custom House for the formal surrender. In keeping with the bilingual traditions of Monterey, the American commodore's proclamation was also read in Spanish, in an attempt to reassure the sullen crowd that had gathered to watch the proceedings.

At the close of the formal ceremony, the troops dutifully raised their voices in the traditional "three cheers for California," while the guns of the Pacific Squadron thundered out a twenty-one gun salute over the capital. As the flag of the United States of America fluttered over the Custom House, the company marched down Calle Principal to the stirring music of naval bandsmen. Mexican dominion over Alta California had ended. At a dinner in Larkin's honor, aboard the American flagship, the conversation centered around the land that was now part of the new American expansionism.

The transition to American statehood was accomplished without the usual trauma of occupation by a conquering nation. Within a week of Sloat's bloodless victory at Monterey, the homes of the leading private citizens were opened to officers of the fleet. Larkin and the Yankee merchants were ecstatic about the new business coming to their port from the American ships, and the young señoritas flirted openly with the robust American marines.

At El Cuartel, construction was begun to renovate the buildings that had been the one civil glory of Alvarado's last administration. A garrison of four hundred men was installed in government houses. A new stockade and a blockhouse were erected at a pace that amazed the slow-moving Californians. An atmosphere of victory, not defeat, permeated the town. The possibilities of expansionism and exploitation of the abundant resources fired a new sense of ambition and imagination. Monterey was no longer an isolated Mexican colonial port on the desolate western coast of the Americas.

Then, suddenly, double columns of rough-looking, bearded freebooters rode into Monterey. At the head of the troops was Captain John Charles Fremont.

While his men camped in a pine forest near the ocean, Fremont parleyed with Commodore Sloat, who was stunned at the brash and irresponsible statements of the American engineering officer. Since Captain Fremont acted in combat on his own authority, without orders from Washington, Commodore Sloat was perplexed about how to negotiate with him. After a restless night, Sloat solved his dilemma by abruptly passing the command of the United States Squadron of the Pacific to his colleague, Commodore Robert F. Stockton. The decision warmed Fremont's heart, since he and Stockton had already sealed the fate of the Californians in a battle plan that would advance both their careers. For Fremont, the bright future included candidacy for president of the United States.

TO THE RELIEF of all in the former capital, Fremont and Stockton soon left the peaceful occupied port of Monterey. Stockton sought to subdue the interior of California by pursuing Castro and Pico, who had retreated through the interior to Los Angeles. Fremont, now a major, sailed with the Americans for San Diego and Los Angeles, where the combined forces sought to trap General Castro and his vaquero army in an attack from both land and sea.

Unfortunately, the Americans had no knowledge of the disposition of the *compañeros* (citizens) of Los Angeles. The pueblo, though outwardly quiet and passive, had for some time been a hotbed of sedition and revolution. The territory had its share of knights-errant who plotted against whoever was in power and dashed about the countryside with pistols and laurel-wood lances like characters from a medieval romance. At night, the *bodegas* of Los Angeles filled with wine-besotted conversation of conspirators plotting revenge against the petty tyrannies of Archibald Gillespie, the American naval captain who had occupied Los Angeles.

On September 22, 1846, at three o'clock in the morning, a party of sixty-five Californians rose in revolt against the government stronghold. For over a week, Serbula Valeras and his comrades, under General José María Flores and Don Andres Pico, with six hundred horsemen and one brass cannon, tried to cut off Gillespie's supply lines. The Americans held their ground with long rifles but were eventually overcome by superior numbers. Even an heroic eleventh-hour ride to Monterey for reinforcements by John Brown, who galloped almost six hundred miles in five days, failed to save Gillespie. On September 30, the Americans surrendered, on the condition that they be allowed to evacuate their garrison by sea from San Pedro to Monterey.

Throughout the fall of 1846, the revolt under the leadership of Don Andres Pico and General Flores spread from San Diego, north, to the ranchos at Santa Barbara. This threat to annexation invited a major American offensive, and by November, General Stephen W. Kearny's Army of the West was marching doggedly on San Diego to repay the Californian insurrectionists. Kearny's four hundred battle-weary men had just achieved victories over Mexican forces in the Southwest. The stage was now set for California's involvement in the Mexican-American War.

In December 1846, as Kearny reached Rancho San Pascual Valley, Pico's vaquero squadron, with lances gleaming in the winter sunlight, swept down upon the Americans from the surrounding hills. In the panic of the first minutes, General Kearny was lanced three times in the arm and buttocks, and one of his howitzers was lassoed by the Californians and hauled back into the hills surrounding the valley. According to Kearny's second-in-command, eighteen Americans were killed and thirteen wounded in the first charge at San Pascual. Only one of the Californians was killed and twelve were wounded, in spite of Kearny's two-to-one superiority. The situation looked desperate for the Americans, who had been routed and pinned down by a troop of vaqueros armed only with wooden lances. But when news reached Andres Pico that reinforcements had been summoned from San Diego by the legendary scout Kit Carson, Pico faded back into the hills and ranchos with his men.

The valiant Pico continued to fight classic holding actions, first at Paseo de Bartola and finally at La Mesa, until January 10, when Gillespie, accompanied by Fremont, returned to raise the flag over Southern California. Alta California was now consolidated under the occupational government of the United States.

Gold
and the Constitution

Colton Hall, about 1890

A S THE HIJOS DEL PAÍS MADE THEIR LAST STAND on the winter plains of Southern California, American leadership was altering the course, if not the character, of old Monterey. A new and eloquent voice spoke out for the preservation of native Californian traditions in the American social and political order. In 1846, Walter Colton, a naval chaplain on the U.S.S. *Congress* and a Congregational clergyman from Vermont, had been appointed as the first American chief administrator of Monterey, a post he held until 1848. This forty-nine-year-old minister, a Yale man and former newspaper editor, brought an open-minded, Jeffersonian intelligence to the insular frontier culture. Colton soon fell in love with all aspects of California, a land that seemed to to him to be a new Arcadia on the shores of the Pacific.

Reverend Walter Colton

COLTON'S ACCOMPLISHMENTS mirrored his wide range of interests and talents — from journalism and social reform to the study of Greek law. He viewed the life-style of dolce far niente as a social refinement and humanism, which pioneer Americans had lost in their selfish lust for wealth. Along with a seven-foot Kentuckian, Robert Semple, Colton founded the *Californian*, the first newspaper published in both English and Spanish.

Colton's civil administration was a model of efficiency and Puritan perfection. Under his enlightened stewardship, bodegas and grogshops were closed on Sunday, gambling was taxed to support the construction of public buildings, and the law was enforced with equanimity and mercy. For a brief moment, Monterey came alive again with an energy born in the tranquility and grace of an earlier time.

During the winter of 1846, Colton's program of peaceful transition and humanitarian reform was rudely interrupted by the return of the recently promoted Colonel Fremont. As Fremont established his headquarters outside Monterey, he immediately commandeered horses on which to mount new recruits to fight in Southern California. In retaliation for the outright theft of their property, the old hijo del país Manuel Castro and a small contingent of vaqueros made an unsuccessful attempt to ambush Fremont's party near Isaac Graham's former distillery at Natividad. After a brief but bloody skirmish in which the Californians suffered severe losses, Castro's force retreated to Rancho los Vergeles, near San Juan Bautista. There they found the American consul, Thomas O. Larkin, on his way to visit his youngest child, who was mortally ill in San Francisco. In the middle of the night, Larkin was taken hostage to the Castro rancho outside Monterey. But the Americans were unable to free Larkin from the enemy camp; Fremont and his men had left the area and were galloping through the winter rains of the Salinas Valley, sacking and looting ranchos that lay between the spinelike ridges of the coastal mountains. It was two months before the American consul was set free and learned of the death of his daughter.

After the surrender at Cahuenga Pass on January 13, 1847, Colton was having his difficulties. The inflationary economy had created food shortages and high prices. The usually abundant supplies of meat from the ranchos had been severely depleted by Fremont's ravaging of cattle and stores. To heighten the tension, neither Fremont nor Kearny acknowledged the military authority of the other. Their bitter feud, displayed in public before the sensitive and always gracious Californians, was eventually resolved by Washington when General Kearny was ordered to arrest and remove Fremont from California.

Thus, in the nation's capital, Fremont, the "Great Pathfinder" of the western frontier, endured the humiliation of a court-martial for mutiny. Fremont left behind the legacy of a sour business relationship with his friend Larkin. He had misdirected three thousand dollars to buy Rancho las Mariposas from a desperate Juan Bautista Alvarado, a transaction that outraged all parties concerned.

The Reverend Walter Colton departed Monterey for an assignment at the Philadelphia Navy Yard, where he wrote his classic work, *Three Years in California*, which was published in 1850, a year before he died of tuberculosis. The great alcalde's vision of a better life was reflected in the writings about his beloved California, and in the neoclassic architecture of Colton Hall, a public building that stands today in the city of Monterey.

44

THE END of the Mexican-American War on February 2, 1848, initially caused both the press and the public to ignore an event that would change California forever. On January 24, gold had been discovered in the foothills of the Sierra Nevada. No longer would the provinces of Sonoma and Sacramento, or Yerba Buena Village on San Francisco Bay, remain isolated from American influence. Nor would Monterey remain the only city of the California territory.

At first, the discovery was ignored by the populace of the northern provinces. But as spring passed into summer, the Golconda in the red earth at Sutter's Mill heralded the beginning of a great western migration. Suddenly, pikers, cardsharps, murderers, drunkards, and thousands of self-styled argonauts were drawn to the magical place called "El Dorado." San Francisco became a seaport overnight, and the well-ordered capital at Monterey, which had flourished under the guiding hand of Walter Colton, was soon reduced to a non-productive adobe pueblo of women, children, and old men.

At the presidio, Colonel Richard Mason, whose command included a young lieutenant named William Tecumseh Sherman, was confronted with a situation approaching anarchy. Soldiers, seamen, and merchants alike were deserting en masse to the Gold Country, as the cry "El Dorado" echoed through the port of old Monterey. By fall 1848, the discharge of the New York Volunteers had left Monterey and San Francisco with only two companies of professional soldiers to guard the guns and keep the peace.

In their Sierra mining camps, men in red flannel shirts no longer tolerated a colonial system dictated by military governors and newly Americanized alcaldes. Only the cooler heads of men like Vallejo, Semple, and Sutter held the ideal of constitutional government above the lust for gold. The spring of 1849 signaled an escalation of the gold rush that pushed against the western shores of California like a human tidal wave. Without a counterbalance for the avarice that was the driving force behind the western migration, California would soon have been overcome with violence and anarchy.

But the nightmare did not materialize. In Washington, President Zachary Taylor, holding the destiny of Monterey in the fragile parchment of the Constitution, dispatched a new governor, Brigadier General Bennett Riley, to form a government in California.

GOVERNOR RILEY LOST NO TIME in calling for a constitutional convention. Together with Thomas King, special envoy from the president, he rode the foothills of the Sierra, rallying the miners to the cause of statehood. The populist concern and grassroots campaigning of the two men paid off with the successful election of delegates to a constitutional convention to be held in September. It was a proper tribute to Walter Colton that the site of the forty-eight-member convention was Colton Hall in Monterey.

Robert Semple, the huge Kentucky frontiersman, was elected to preside over a membership that reflected the larger population of the north. Of the thirty-eight northern representatives, many were lawyers or merchants. Eight were Californians, only one of whom had been elected from the local land-grant ranchos; the hijos del país politely ignored the governmental proceedings of los Americanos. Yet many of the major political figures of the decade were present at Colton Hall to argue, to inveigh, and finally to compromise.

William Hartnell, the aging educator who became known as "Don Guillermo," translated for los Californianos. The American point of view was championed by John Sutter, Thomas Larkin, Charles Halleck, Abel Stearns, William Gwin, Robert Semple, and Bennett Riley. The most eloquent voice was that of the great democrat Mariano Guadalupe Vallejo, who, in spite of an imprisonment by Semple in the past, was a staunch advocate of statehood.

At the convention, some of the issues were decided swiftly. Slavery was unanimously voted down, and through the efforts of Morton McCarver, a placer miner, blacks were allowed to work the gold mines free from the indenture of Southern owners. Other issues were not so unanimously resolved. Californians with Native American ancestry were granted suffrage, subject to a future amendment approved by two-thirds of the legislature.

And, as was to become traditional in California politics, the land itself became the central issue. Halleck and Gwin argued for a state that extended east, to Salt Lake, while Sutter, Pablo de la Guerra, and Jacinto Rodríguez demanded the high desert of Nevada as their domain. The constitutional president, Robert Semple, held out for topographic distribution along the Colorado River and the eastern slope of the Sierra Nevada.

The final majority voted with the cool logic of commom sense. Too large a land mass would prevent a stubborn, divided Congress in Washington from reaching a prompt vote for statehood. The rational compromise was to limit the boundaries to the edge of the Sierra's eastern slope down the leg of present-day California, to the desert borders of Mexico and Arizona. The die was cast. Six weeks after Semple's keynote speech calling for "justice, industry, and economy," the constitutional convention of California declared itself adjourned.

Old Monterey celebrated in a stylized choreography of manners, dance, and song. American backwoodsmen, miners, army officers, merchants, and Hispanophiles all rejoiced in the embrace of the hijos del país. A new optimism filled the Indian summer night, falling like gold dust on the old capital. The streets were full of idealism and a sense of destiny that united the two cultures of old Monterey. The delegates congratulated themselves with generous stipends of silver from the Civil Fund, and the famous artist, journalist, and world traveler J. Ross Browne received a commission of ten thousand dollars to print his official report of the proceedings.

On October 12, 1849, the leading citizens of the province gathered at a lavish ball — hosted by the delegates to the convention — honoring the great event that had transpired. The celebration was both the culmination of two decades of turmoil and Monterey's adiós to the glories of its gentle past.

A Land for Sale

ON SEPTEMBER 9, 1850, the Congress of the United States hastily admitted California into the Union, without territorial probation. Washington acted with unprecedented speed. To many of the desperate men and women who came to San Francisco in clipper ships and covered wagons, the golden treasure at the end of the great western rainbow seemed an hallucinatory encounter with their own mortality. Pestilence and despair haunted the hovels and shanties of the Gold Country, and for every cry of "Eureka!" or "Bonanza!" muffled curses rose from the multitudes who had "seen the elephant" and failed.

Although there is no accurate way of knowing how many persons came to California during the gold rush years, the population of some twenty thousand at statehood grew to more than one million by the time of the last Comstock Lode silver bonanza, almost thirty years later. Under the leadership of the visionary banker, William Chapman Ralston, the sand dunes of Yerba Buena Village became a Pacific metropolis on the hills by San Francisco Bay.

IN MONTEREY, although the economy of the old capital had slowed to a depressed state, many of the aging citizens seemed unperturbed by the social and political upheaval created by the gold rush. In 1856, the California legislature passed an amendment to the city charter authorizing trustees to sell, if necessary, all the city land in Monterey to pay the cost of title confirmation. In a few short years, the old romantic capital had become a quiet ruin, a bankrupt adobe pueblo with only one remaining element of legitimate commerce — shore whaling.

The first whaling company, known as the "Old Company," was organized in 1854 to harvest the humpback and the California gray whale as they migrated to breeding grounds in Baja.

Early hunting methods were primitive — whalers hurled rusty harpoons into the heaving sides of humpbacks. Later, bomb lances and harpoon guns began to kill with increasing accuracy in the blue-gray waters along the Monterey Coast. The giant mammals always put up a gallant fight for survival, and often their huge, fifty-foot-long bodies surfaced in their death agonies to smash the boats of the whalers who had tormented them. Still, the defenseless whales were no match for the whalers. The sight of a stripped whale carcass alongside a foul-smelling cluster of huge copper kettles and furnaces became commonplace on the shores of Monterey Bay. Whaling companies boasted that they were the sole support of the economy of Monterey.

By the late 1870s, annual production of whale oil harvested from the slaughter of females and their young, returning from breeding grounds in Baja, reached four thousand barrels. The task of whaling was made easier by the knowledge that once a calf was struck by a harpoon, the mother cow would never desert her offspring. Fortunately, the slaughter of the humpback and the gray whale was at last slowed by public acceptance of mineral oil and by the decrease in the number of whales..

The Whale Harvest, 1872

50

O N THE BOUNTIFUL RANCHOS that surrounded the impoverished capital, life still had a tempered, quiet ambiance. Time, like the ranchos, seemed to have no boundary. Along the gentle Salinas and Carmel rivers, old California families continued their fiestas in the last mellow days of dolce far niente.

John Charles and Jesse Fremont, now private citizens of California, returned, after Fremont's court-martial for mutiny, to play out fantasies of Renaissance nobility in the subculture of old California. The arrogant past was somehow forgotten in the extravagantly theatrical life-style they fashioned for themselves as the first family of a California society emerging around San Francisco Bay. Old enemies finally accepted Fremont as one of their own, as *muy simpático*, for they found in the American a kindred spirit who had adopted the California way of life.

But in 1851, three thousand miles east in Washington, the fate of Fremont and his neighbors was being determined. The United States Land Commission, a result of the Treaty of Guadalupe Hidalgo, which ended the Mexican-American War, challenged every land-grant title in California. Thousands of acres were held up for confirmation or rejection. Although some of the land had been carved to bits as *caballeros* gambled away portions of their ranchos in the saloons of Salinas, now all huge tracts of land were in danger of being completely lost. Families who had been unable or had simply forgotten to pay their taxes became vulnerable to anyone with enough cash to pay the delinquent debt and take title to their land. So it passed that even Fremont, co-author, with his wife, of a best-selling book on his exploration of Oregon and California, and a candidate for the presidency of the United States, was forced off the land like many of his ranchero friends.

In this new era of real estate, much of the Salinas Valley was quietly bought up by an unassuming Italian tinsmith named Alberto Trescony. After arriving in Monterey in 1842, Trescony lived in a tin shack and made his living by creating cups from cast-off tin cans that he received from the town's housewives. When he shrewdly turned from making tin cups to fashioning tin pans for the gold rush miners at thirty-five dollars apiece, the Italian soon made a considerable fortune. Eventually, he accumulated enough money to buy the forty thousand-acre Rancho Tulacitos, as well as two other thriving enterprises — the Washington Hotel in Monterey and Deacon Howe's Halfway House in Salinas.

Patiently, the lonely tinsmith waited for equal success in love. The woman of his heart, a New Zealander named Catherine Cotton Rainey, unfortunately already had a husband. Although his romance with her flourished, Trescony had little hope for marriage. Desperately unhappy with her abusive husband, Catherine was finally released from her bonds of marriage in return for a large sum of money from Trescony to Mr. Rainey. The joyful couple bought the Rancho San Lucas in the Salinas Valley on which to raise their family. In time, the gentle Italian became one of the most beloved ranchers in the valley.

Washington Hotel, about 1890

ALTHOUGH ALBERTO TRESCONY managed to accumulate huge landholdings by legitimate purchase from rancho families around Monterey, other entrepreneurs were less honest in their dealings. One of the most notorious individuals obsessed with the golden opportunities of real estate was the stocky Scotsman David Jacks. Taking advantage of the naiveté of the Californians and their lack of business acumen, Jacks managed to carve out a substantial portion of the surrounding countryside for himself. Often, he would make cash loans to the rancho families, knowing that they could never hope to repay him except with their land. More frequently, Jacks simply paid the back taxes and took title to the property of families who would then make their shocking discovery in court. More than one hijo del país took a shot at Jacks, who traveled with a bodyguard and never dared to take a meal in public for fear of poison. Perhaps his most cold-blooded purchase was the forced sale of Hartnell's beloved Rancho El Alisal by Hartnell's widow for a mere one hundred twenty-two dollars.

Jacks' acquisitiveness did not stop with that purchase. In 1859, the city of Monterey was forced to auction off part of its landholdings in order to pay legal fees to attorney Delos Ashley, who had successfully defended the city's title against the United States Land Commission. The little-publicized auction drew only two bidders, David Jacks and his friend Delos Ashley. For just over one thousand dollars, the two men bought up thirty thousand acres of Monterey pueblo and presidio lands. Irate citizens, when they finally learned of the quiet dealings, filed suit against Jacks all the way to the United States Supreme Court. However, the final judgment was in favor of Jacks. By the late 1800s, Jacks held title to sixty thousand acres in Monterey County and owned ten former land grant properties.

At the same time, Charles Crocker's Southern Pacific Railroad opened the Monterey Peninsula to development from San Francisco and the east. Not to be outdone by Crocker's operations, the aging David Jacks constructed his own narrow-gauge railway to undercut the shipping charges of Southern Pacific.

Jacks' enterprise, which was in turn underpriced by Southern Pacific, failed miserably. But Crocker's railroad flourished and brought thousands of visitors from around the world to the Monterey Coast.

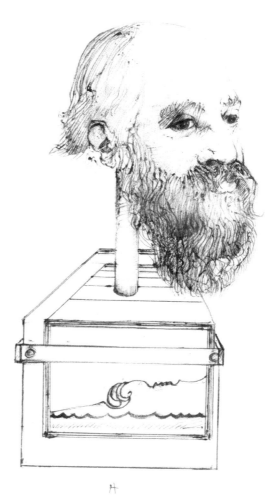

David Jacks

54

Artists, Writers, and Environmentalists

56

The Gathering

"Any good mixer of convivial habits considers he has a right to be called a Bohemian. But this is not a valid claim. There are two elements, at least, that are essential to Bohemianism. The first is the devotion or addiction to one or more of the Seven Arts; the other is poverty."
— (Attributed to George Sterling)
Franklin Walker, *The Seacoast of Bohemia*

N O HOTEL, IT WAS SAID, could survive in the generous atmosphere of Monterey's Hispanic past. Yet by 1879, several modest hostelries, including the St. Charles and the French hotels, offered time-honored pleasures. Delight in ceremony accompanied by simple courtesy lived on during the declining years of dolce far niente, in small inns and restaurants such as the Sánchez Saloon and Jules Simoneau's marvelous French eating establishment.

In the late 1870s, Simoneau's had become a nightly gathering place for a small, ragged cast of bohemian artists, writers, and journalists, who crowded together over local brandy and California vin ordinaire.

The term "bohemian" was not used in the traditional sense of nineteenth-century Paris. Instead, California's brand of bohemianism was to become a metaphor for life among the gifted and not-so-gifted artists and writers of the time. George Sterling, the first poet laureate of California, who was later to lead a pilgrimage to the Monterey Coast, defined this new style of life.

In old Monterey, the first wave of bohemian artists — Joe Strong and the French painters Julian Rix and Jules Travernier — joined other immigrants for discussion in Simoneau's steamy room on Tyler Street. The fading adobe town of Monterey held a past, a nostalgia, a smell of ruins that was quite different from the bonanza newness and energy of San Francisco. No matter that the town was nearly abandoned by the Americans. No matter that the guitars and Spanish voices in the night air were softer, older, and more removed from reality than those of the gold rush capital. These men were refugees from failed careers and a decadent Europe, or from the bustling metropolis to the north.

Jules Simoneau was a kindly, bearded, old Frenchman, who relished chess and the company of any who practiced — or pretended to practice — the art of belles lettres. He was a man at once refined and careless of material wealth. The old man was often a benefactor to newcomers who made their way down El Camino Real by stagecoach or to those who arrived aboard the passenger coach of the narrow-gauge Monterey and Salinas Valley Railroad. On the last day of August 1879, Simoneau met yet another bohemian, this time an "amateur emigrant," as he called himself, from the highlands of Scotland. His name was Robert Louis Stevenson.

Robert Louis Stevenson

STEVENSON ARRIVED IN MONTEREY, a place he called "the Old Pacific Capital," at the age of twenty-nine, impoverished and hopelessly in love with a woman who was still married to another man. It was a romantic adventure that, happily, was later consummated in marriage. An unknown and disinherited Stevenson was obsessed with an Oakland woman named Fanny Vandegrift Osbourne, ten years his senior, whom he had met in the French town Grez Sur Loing. Their legendary romance had ended in Paris, when Mr. Osborne refused to support his estranged wife unless she returned home to the San Francisco Bay Area. When Fanny's illness resulted in a final separation from her husband, she moved to cheap quarters on Alvarado Street in Monterey, and Stevenson, half-dead with tuberculosis himself, borrowed the fare for an emigrant-class crossing that would take him to California for a rendezvous with his future wife.

Robert Louis Stevenson's four months in Monterey became a battle for survival in the rooming houses along Calle Principal. At first, the young writer endured eviction by the granddaughter of Mariano Guadalupe Vallejo, who feared that the young man's eczema and consumption would contaminate her chilly adobe boarding house with a fatal disease. This selfish act by the old harridan set the tone for Stevenson's unhappy sojourn in the dim rooms of Monterey. Stevenson's experience was in marked contrast to Jules Simoneau's hospitality and to the traditions of Old California. Nevertheless, the torment and the pain in his lungs could not break the artist's resolve to write books.

In two months, Stevenson finished a short story entitled "The Pavilion on the Links" and immersed himself in *The Amateur Emigrant*, a tale of his pilgrimage to California. But the killing pace of his work in cold rooms and his despondency over Fanny's marital situation depressed his spirit until he collapsed while on a camping trip in Carmel Valley.

For the remainder of his time in Monterey, Stevenson spent afternoons in Fanny Osbourne's rose garden on Alvarado Street, where he read for the criticism of the Osbourne children, Fanny's sister, Nellie, and the great lady herself. Then the young writer would adjourn to the more relaxed atmosphere of Jules Simoneau's restaurant, where he became a member in good standing of the first bohemian conclave on the Monterey Coast.

Stevenson also grew fond of wandering in the wooded hills, often finding peace and inspiration in the quiet ambiance of what later became Del Monte Forest. The Carmel mission had fallen to ruin, with little remaining besides the church facade and its solitary tower. "The church is roofless and ruinous," Stevenson wrote, "with sea-breezes and sea-fogs, and the alternation of rain and sunshine, daily widening the breaches and casting crockets from the wall." His walks took him far from the beach, across the mouth of Carmel River to Point Lobos, with its strange red lichen, rockbound coves, and windswept, twisted cypress that gave the promontory the mystical look of an ancient Chinese scroll. Years later, this wild coast made its appearance in world literature as the dramatic surround for *Treasure Island*.

As winter rains approached and the damp fog covered the old capital, Stevenson was stricken with pneumonia in his dingy room at Madame Girardin's French Hotel on Mission Street. Fortunately, since the little inn was near Simoneau's restaurant, Stevenson received daily hot broths. The ministering of Simoneau and his wife literally brought him back to life. When the stubborn young Scot raised himself to continue writing, he collapsed again in weakness — this time to the consternation of Madame Girardin, who tolerated no illness at her cheap establishment. A sick roomer, it seemed, was bad for business. After brief treatment by Dr. Heinz, the good madame's son-in-law, Stevenson's recuperation continued in more hospitable climes near San Francisco.

In December 1879, the Osbourne clan, with Robert Louis Stevenson in tow, departed their rooms on Alvarado Street. The young man, on the verge of his first success, was happy to leave. "The tattling town" had accused him of setting fire to the forest, fathering an illegitimate child in the image of Fanny Osbourne's son Lloyd, and contaminating the houses of Monterey with disease. But his friends at Simoneau's, the artists and other bohemians, were sad to see their sickly but uncomplaining friend leave. Though he predicted that the "native gentlemen of Monterey must perish, like a lower race, before the millionaire vulgarians of the 'Big Bonanza,'" Stevenson's *Old Pacific Capital* became a classic description of old Monterey.

Castro Adobe in 1887

60

The Del Monte

INSPIRED BY WILLIAM CHAPMAN RALSTON'S magnificent Palace Hotel in San Francisco, Charles Crocker embarked on the construction of what was one of the great seaside resorts of the time. The Del Monte, a five hundred-room, wooden Victorian hotel in Monterey, rose from the land like a sun-washed California version of the great European spa-resorts. It was built in less than a year at a cost of more than one million dollars. Its heated salt-water swimming pools, the elegant rooms and service, and its thousand gas lights eventually repaid the railroad tycoon's investment many times over.

The Del Monte was an overnight sensation. Soon the fabulous hotel attracted the attention of the rich and worldly citizens of the Victorian Age and it became fashionable to ride the new full-gauge branch line of the Southern Pacific Railroad to Monterey, to take the waters, and to toast each other's good fortune with champagne at Charles Crocker's Hotel Del Monte. The new sybarite-pilgrims arrived with parasols and in tallyhos to gaze at each other under the sun. They celebrated a living theater of opulence that flourished in Victorian summers by the sea. Within the bounds of an ornamental cypress hedge that contained a luminous mass of gardens, voluptuous ladies in white dresses

61

Waiting for the Del Monte Express

and their portly, silk-hatted escorts revived the flirtatious, courtly rites of an earlier age. But now there were no guitars or scented *cascarones* (eggshells filled with gold dust and lavender for a favored señorita). The old Pacific capital was a quaint tourist attraction, a relic from the past, a decorative, historic tableau for guests to see as they rode by in open carriages like figures in a French impressionist painting.

When the great Hotel Del Monte burned down in 1888, without loss of life, a larger, three-storied variation on the original architectural theme rose in its place to give expression to the expansive Californian society of the 1890s. The new Del Monte mirrored the vulgarity and excesses of the Bonanza days in Virginia City and San Francisco, catering to the insatiable appetites of railroad kings. Along with the guests, tons of meat

arrived daily on the Del Monte Express, and wagonloads of produce from Carmel Valley provided for the cavernous new banquet halls, where nearly a thousand people could feast at one sitting. This ritual, designed to make mortals feel like gods, was but a distant reminder of the fiestas of old California. In the 1890s, the resort community obscured the spirit of an earlier time in the mirrored theatricality of the Victorian Age.

At the Del Monte, a polo field, a race track, and a golf course graced the shoreline of what was part of a successful real estate development. The Crocker resort empire grew so large and was so self-contained that it published a newspaper called the *Del Monte Wave*.

David Starr Jordan, soon to become the first president of Stanford University, surveyed the small bay at the headlands of

the Carmel River for the 1880 census. Jordan later described Carmel Beach in glowing prose — both in his government report on its aquatic life and in an article for *Scribner's Monthly* in New York. Jordan was also certain that California's new land-and-tourism boom would logically extend over the hill from the Hotel Del Monte toward Carmel Valley. And inland from the bay, the Carmel mission was showing signs of life. Thanks to restoration work, the sanctuary had been cleared to reveal the burial place of Junípero Serra, Fermín Francisco de Lasuén, and Juan Crespí. Restoration brought new pride in California's heritage to a society lacking a sense of purpose or an understanding of its past. This new excitement and interest in a regional past were not lost on Carmel developer S.F. Duckworth.

By 1888, Duckworth had purchased a section of Rancho las Manzanitas in an attempt to establish a Catholic summer community similar to the successful Methodist Chautauqua retreat in nearby Pacific Grove. He printed a brochure, sold two hundred lots near the upper northern slope of Ocean Avenue, and hastily built a small hotel near Junípero Street and Ocean to entice discriminating tourists. But a Catholic summer retreat never materialized, and the Southern Pacific Railroad showed no signs of expansion over the hill to Carmel. Duckworth's twenty dollar lots went begging, and the depression of the early 1890s did little to save him from bankruptcy. Six years after the first lots had been sold, during the California land boom of the 1880s, Carmel became a yellowing design on a land developer's map.

Along Monterey Bay, a fishing community of Chinese, fugitives from the chaos of China at midcentury, settled in villages in order to harvest the wealth of the sea. As the Ohlone before them, they "lived lightly on the land." Their diet, disciplined by centuries of hardship, included varieties of plants and sea creatures foreign to the western palate. And dried abalone, kelp, and squid soon found a market in China, at a time when Western merchants claimed that only opium was profitable enough to balance China trade.

The fishing villages maintained themselves on the periphery of the Monterey economy, in the face of continual challenge from Italian and Portuguese commercial fishermen and from the racist limitations of the Chinese Exclusion Act.

By 1890, the Chinese population, including fishermen, farmers, laborers, and entrepreneurs, numbered over sixteen hundred people — almost ten percent of the population of Monterey County. But this population was to drop drastically after 1910.

The Chinese did not pose either social or economic threat to the new American community. Their most important village was Point Alones on the rocky shore between today's Monterey Bay Aquarium and the Hopkins Marine Station. To the westerner, the cemetery and shrines, the sampans and omnipresent smell of dried squid suggested a fishing village on the coast of China.

After the turn of the century, the pressure to open waterfront property to real estate development signaled an end to this picturesque view of another culture. Then in 1906, a fire burned out Point Alones, and although the Pacific Improvement Company had been a benign landlord, the village was not rebuilt.

The now-barren site was acquired by Stanford University, and the Chinese soon dispersed to other Chinatowns scattered throughout the region. The new century brought competition from Sicilian and Japanese fishermen, and by 1930, only one Chinese commercial fisherman remained on the Monterey Coast.

Touring the Carmel Coast

The Old Doña

66

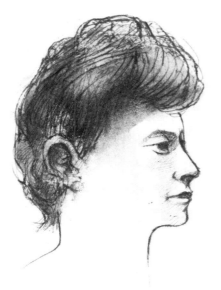

*I*N LITERATURE, the romance and illusion of old California and the glorious dream of dolce far niente lived on in the work of certain novelists. A beautiful and ambitious young widow, who had lived at Rancho Valparaiso on the peninsula south of San Francisco, wrote of these epochal days. Gertrude Atherton, a native of San Francisco, had returned from a tour of Europe and New York to chronicle life on the ranchos of early California. In her short-story collections, *Before the Gringo Came* and *The Splendid Idle Forties*, and in the novel *Rezanov*, Atherton revealed an aristocrat's nostalgia for the lost utopian mission era.

As a matter of course, Gertrude Atherton frequently visited the environs of her heroines to gather local color for her stories and novels that described the Spanish traditions of old Monterey.

In *Patience Sparhawk and Her Times*, Atherton presented a powerful account of a lonely rebel who haunted the crags of Point Lobos and climbed the crumbling bell tower of Mission San Carlos Borromeo. The psychological distortion of the characters and the dreamlike violence of the plot revealed a darker side of the coastal ambiance. Something fearful, almost deathlike, lay embedded in the underwater jade forests of the sea beyond Lobos. *Patience* was a sensation when it was first published in England in 1897, where critics hailed the novelist for her story of a California woman. Suddenly, the Monterey Coast had become a colorful, romantic background for art.

During the fin de siècle years, as bohemianism had become the fashion in San Francisco, artists and poets had gathered in the vicinity of North Beach known as the "Monkey Block." Then, gradually, a rise in rents began to drive the bohemians from this legendary quarter. Many of these young, displaced men and women eventually looked south to Carmel for a haven. Some had visited old Monterey. They remembered Simoneau's or the Sánchez Saloon or had walked the white beaches to Point Lobos along trails blazed by Robert Louis Stevenson. Others were more desperate, confronted by the hard reality of staying alive while practicing the art that was their true metier.

Over the hill from the Del Monte and old Monterey, a new resort development called Carmel-by-the-Sea took hold on the sandy slopes of Ocean Avenue. Kindly old James Franklin Devendorf, who owned subdivisions as far away as San Jose and Stockton, traded for an eighty-acre tract set back from Carmel Beach. With the backing of San Francisco lawyer, Frank Powers, he acquired additional property. By 1903, the Carmel Development Company was chartered.

Early Photograph of Carmel-by-the-Sea

The Devendorf-Powers venture was in marked contrast to Duckworth's disastrous get-rich-quick attempt at exploiting the restoration of Mission San Carlos Borromeo. The developers of Carmel-by-the-Sea were patient businessmen who saw substantial profit in the aesthetic beauty of their investment. Erosion on Ocean Avenue was forestalled by planting trees both in the middle of the avenue and on the bald, nearby slopes. Duckworth's hotel was transported five blocks down the hill, where it formed the central structure of what is today the Pine Inn.

On the Fourth of July 1903, the refurbished Carmel Inn opened to boisterous and enthusiastic crowds from the San Joaquin Valley, and the new era of Carmel-by-the-Sea began. Tents for summer guests were erected at the rear of the inn, and lots were offered for one hundred dollars apiece, on terms of five dollars down and five dollars a month. Potential buyers, referred by Powers in San Francisco, endured the hour-long haul over the hill from the Southern Pacific station in Monterey, destination point of the crack Del Monte Express. Within the year, the village boasted a permanent population of thirty-two families, and more than seventy-five wooden cabins nestled in the sandy ruts and piney nooks of the forest north of Ocean Avenue.

Soon Carmel-by-the-Sea was to become known as a place of seacoast and self-sufficiency. The sea air, the muffled pounding of the surf, the early morning light as fog lifted over Point Lobos, and the pale tones of amber, rose, and turquoise in the illuminated afterglow of the heavens, conjured up an eternal image of an American paradise on the Pacific. It was an image that artists and writers could not resist.

George Sterling

Abalone Song

AT THIRTY-SIX, GEORGE STERLING was the leader of that small but select group of artists, writers, and journalists who formed the nucleus of San Francisco's Bohemian Club. Sterling was born at Sag Harbor, on Long Island Sound. His physician father had converted the family to Roman Catholicism in time for George to study briefly at St. Charles Seminary near Baltimore. Just as his brother had assumed the vows of priesthood, Sterling always retained a symbolic connection to the church by his self-image of poet-as-priest. Throughout his life, Sterling abstained from profanity, tobacco, and coffee. Yet, to compensate for such discipline, he freely allowed himself the pleasures of women and wine.

After moving west to Piedmont, across the bay from San Francisco, Sterling worked steadily at the thriving insurance brokerage of his uncle, Frank C. Havens, in the City. Soon Sterling had married Carrie Rand, a stunning wasp-waisted "Gibson Girl," formerly a stenographer at the same office. On the surface, Sterling was the perfect image of a businessman. But this staid, bourgeois facade covered a frantic inner energy that later led him to throw off his respectability in a Gauguinesque rebellion of art for art's sake.

Each day, on the ferry to San Francisco, the young poet lost himself in rhymes and word images that eventually formed the basis of his introverted, neoclassical style. His early work was composed as a release from the conformity and frustration of a job he hated. Then, through his association with the cynical and powerful critic Ambrose Bierce, Sterling began to publish his poems in the local press.

Naturally generous and ingratiating, Sterling was a charming host, and he became part of the crowd that lived in the Berkeley hills: the wildly theatrical Joaquin Miller, self-styled "sweet singer of the Sierras," who affected buckskin and moccasins; Jimmy Hopper, a former California football star turned short-story writer; Blanche Partington, critic for the *San Francisco Call*; Xavier Martinez, the dashing Mexican artist from the Beaux Arts in Paris; and "Fra" Harry Lafler, editor of *The Blue Mule*.

In 1901, George Sterling established what was to be a close friendship with Jack London. "Wolf," as Sterling called the younger — and always more successful — London, lost no time in leading his fellow bohemian, "Greek," through the saloons and flesh emporiums of San Francisco.

Two years later, the friends had achieved literary success. London's *Call of the Wild* was an international best-seller, while Sterling's book of poetry *Testimony of the Suns* was published in the San Francisco Bay Area. Suddenly, the poet's new-found literary career, helped along by his friendships with London and Bierce, brought him local notoriety. When there came an offer from Frank Devendorf of cheap land down the coast, Sterling reasoned that it was time to quit his job for a life of art and self-sufficiency. So it was that Sterling and his wife, Carrie, accompanied by two amateur-carpenter friends, set about building a large redwood lodge, near what is now the Forest Theater.

Joaquin Miller, George Sterling and Charles Warren Stoddard

BY 1906, THE PHOTOGRAPHER Arnold Genthe and Mary Hunter Austin, author of *The Land of Little Rain*, joined Sterling's circle at Carmel-by-the-Sea. Genthe, a German academician, complete with dueling scars, had fallen in love with California and had decided to emigrate. He lived first in San Francisco, where he began photographing leading figures of the region for substantial fees. Thanks to his family connections and a talent for composition that anticipated the art of interpretive portraiture, people flocked to Genthe's Sutter Street studio for sittings. Before long he had money to complete a photo essay on Chinatown and to build his dream studio in Carmel. Genthe's good fortune was also sufficient to subsidize his pioneering work in color photography, using the autochrome process that had been developed by the Lumiere brothers in France. From the basement darkroom under his redwood studio-home in Carmel, Arnold Genthe, classical scholar and frustrated painter, was the first Carmelite to contribute to a popular new artform of the twentieth century. In 1911, an exhibition of his color photographs set technical standards for photographic art in America.

Later, Genthe chronicled life among the Carmel artists' and writers' community in his book *As I Remember*, published in 1936.

Arnold Genthe, Self-Portrait

BANCROFT LIBRARY

Mary Austin

MARY HUNTER AUSTIN, stocky and plain-looking, was the most versatile and talented writer to come to the Monterey Coast during the halcyon days before the Great War. By 1904, when she first arrived in Carmel to research *Isidro*, a novel of old California, the thirty-seven-year-old Austin had already established a modest literary career based on her plays, short stories, and *The Land of Little Rain*. At the insistence of her new-found friend George Sterling, who was both guide and host, the two writers became comrades. The emotional demands of a loveless marriage to an aging schoolmaster and the birth of a retarded daughter in the Owens Valley desert had not prepared her for the experience of the coast. Carmel, in particular, stunned her with its wild shoreline and eerie fog.

No sooner had Mary Austin settled into a small log cabin on North Lincoln Avenue than she placed a platform that she called her "wickiup" in an oak tree behind her home. Each morning she climbed the little wooden ladder to work on a book about shepherds that was to be a companion piece to *The Land of Little Rain*. When she finished her daily routine, she descended to partake of social rituals that evolved about the magnetic presence of George Sterling.

Sterling introduced her to the local literati during evenings around the campfires of Carmel. But such people as Ina Coolbrith and Charles Warren Stoddard, founders of the *Overland Monthly*, and John Muir, Edwin Markham, and Xavier Martinez did not take quickly to Mary Austin. This feisty young woman, who was a year older than her sponsor, was too eccentric for the free-minded intelligentsia. The local community looked askance at the newcomer, who walked the forest dressed in buckskin or draped in the flowing robes of a Greek tragedian. At those genteel soirees, she had the sharpest eye for hypocrisy and literary pretense, and she let others know it.

Occasionally, in the afternoon, Mary Austin and George Sterling hiked from redwood forests down to the sea to savor the mysterious ambiance of the south coast. Sterling, more than Austin, carried this adventure to reckless heights — climbing cliffs or surfing on dangerous waves that sent him tumbling into the breakers. Austin often totally lost sight of him until, down the shoreline, a dark head bobbed up in the foam.

Yet, if George Sterling chose to test his "genius" in combat with nature, Mary Austin seemed never to compulsively court that sting-of-the-senses in order to inspire her own writing. Between them, her passion was not returned in kind.

Later, when the colony of writers and artists had grown larger after the ravages of the San Francisco earthquake, a more exacting routine was agreed on for the Carmel community. "We settled into a habit of morning work which was an anathema to interrupt," reported Mary Austin at the time. "By early afternoon, one and another painter and writer folk could be seen sauntering by piney trails." Then, just before sunset, George Sterling strode down the main street of Carmel, leading a band of motley figures to the white sand below Ocean Avenue. On the beach, fires were lit and a feast of abalone, mussels, wine, and fresh loaves of sourdough bread was prepared to the raucous accompaniment of ballads and dramatic renditions by Mary Austin and her entourage. The abalone song with its endless verses was their favorite:

> *Oh! some folks boast of quail on toast,*
> *Because they think it's tony;*
> *But I'm content to owe my rent*
> *and live on abalone.*
>
> *The more we take, the more they make*
> *In deep-sea matrimony;*
> *Race suicide cannot betide*
> *The fertile abalone.*
>
> *Oh! some think the Lord is fat*
> *And some think He is bony;*
> *But as for me I think that He*
> *Is like an abalone.*

George Sterling often gave abalone or mussel parties on the beach on Sunday afternoons. He and Jimmie Hopper would dive under the deep water by the cliffs and pry the abalones from the rocks. The abalones would then have to undergo an hour's pounding with stones — we all took a hand at it — and after an hour or two of parboiling they would be cut into steaks and broiled on a grill over the open fire. At one of these Mary [Austin] appeared, as she often did, in the beaded leather costume and long braids of an Indian princess. George Sterling, who was proud of his classic contours, had climbed to the top of the cliff in his bathing trunks. Somewhere or other he had procured a trident and he was standing silhouetted against the sky while Jimmy Hopper was taking his picture. This was too frivolous for Mary, who was gazing at the setting sun. Standing on the beach with outstretched arms, she began something which sounded like an incantation, but which turned out to be a quotation from Browning. "It is a Cyclopean blacksmith," chanted Mary, "striking frenzied sparks from the anvil of the horizon." London was standing with a fork in hand, having just disposed of an abalone steak. Taking a look around, which included both Mary and the horizon, he exclaimed, "Hell! I say this sunset has guts!"

— Arnold Genthe, *As I Remember*

George Sterling on the cliff

76

THE PEACEFUL ANARCHY of Carmel was suddenly disturbed by the San Francisco earthquake of April 18, 1906. Although located far from its epicenter, the little seaside community felt the shocks and aftershocks of the quake that devastated the city to the north. Sterling's house lost a chimney, and other Carmelites lost china, but thankfully no one was injured. Arnold Genthe happened to be in San Francisco, where he took historic photographs of the ruins. Mary Austin, in the city to meet with her agent, had left her room at the Palace Hotel the day before the disaster to return home to Carmel-by-the-Sea. She had spent the last day in San Francisco warning her friends of the coming holocaust.

In contrast to a burned-out city, the stunning natural beauty of Carmel Beach provided an interesting backdrop for those who wanted to share Sterling's vision of a New Arcadia on the Pacific Coast. The old Piedmont group — Joaquin Miller, Xavier Martinez, Harry Lafler (now in the company of a beautiful young poet named Nora May French), Jimmy Hopper, and the Partingtons — naturally gravitated to Sterling like bohemian courtiers. Over the hill at Del Monte, an aging Charles Warren Stoddard and the fine painter of the Barbizon-in-California School, Charles Rollo Peters, hosted visiting Carmelites who returned the favor with invitations to elaborate beach parties on the sand dunes that bordered Ocean Avenue.

With Sterling's old friend Jack London in attendance, talk at the beach invariably turned to the international Socialist movement. The ensuing debates and arguments grew to such proportions that Ambrose Bierce rarely visited Carmel, condemning the colony as a hotbed of radicalism. Yet the rhetoric of beach politicians did not deter the establishment from carving out its pieces of Carmel real estate. Substantial-looking summer homes on Camino Real were constructed by refined and dignified professors from Stanford and the University of California at Berkeley. David Starr Jordan, then president of Stanford, built a home at Carmel, and that exquisite patron of San Francisco, James Duval Phelan, motored down the coast in his chauffeured, pearl-white Mercedes-Benz to look things over. The austere outdoorsman John Muir and the early California landscape painter William Keith visited the colony, as did the social reformer Lincoln Steffens, who was later to settle in Carmel.

By 1907, Devendorf's Carmel Development Company expanded its tracts to include part of the Martin Ranch, on what is today Carmel Point, and the population of the town began to increase rapidly.

With London away on a romantic voyage to the South Seas, the summer sun was to fall like a spotlight on George Sterling. The Bohemian Club presented Sterling's play *The Triumph of Bohemia* in the redwoods by the Russian River, and that fall, William Randolph Hearst's *Cosmopolitan* magazine published "A Wine of Wizardry" as its centerpiece.

Accompanying Sterling's poem was an article by Ambrose Bierce. The critic hailed his protégé, by virtue of his reliance on meter and rhyme, as a "very great poet — incomparably the greatest...on this side of the Atlantic." William Randolph Hearst had obviously encouraged Bierce to overpraise the archaic and regional mediocrity of a favorite disciple for the excitement it would cause in New York. The resultant furor would certainly launch his new magazine in a shower of publicity and debate.

Unfortunately, the publication of "A Wine of Wizardry" had little to do with Sterling's talents as a poet. Ina Coolbrith, the poet and librarian who had encouraged Jack London in his youth, more accurately appraised the piece for its obvious weakness, its excess of purple images. Still, the images of "blue-eyed vampires" and "leprous" moons evoked a kind of crazy theatricality that captured the attention of a growing public. And rumors of the poet's insatiable appetite for the opposite sex and of his exploits when he was overcome with wine became part of the Sterling legend. He was at once a cult figure, "the handsome Greek faun" of Mary Austin's description.

Doubtless George Sterling was upset by the embarrassing overstatement that surrounded the publication of his work by Hearst. In letters to Jack London and in conversation with his friends in Carmel, he deplored his fate. Basically shy and introverted, Sterling must have known that he was not yet fit company for the masters of classical poetry. At best, his style and imagery were escapist, caught up in a strange search for antiquity — a preoccupation with some far-off neoplatonic vision of beauty.

That fall, talk on the beach turned invariably to designs for simple-living on the land. It was conversation less sober than the table-talk of the "other" colony, the professors and wealthy summer residents who inhabited Carmel Point. And often, after the autumn sun vanished into the ocean, the talk was of suicide.

George Sterling, Mary Austin, Jack London, and Jimmy Hopper
HARRISON MEMORIAL LIBRARY

Then on November 14, 1907, Nora May French, an intimate member of the Sterling household, killed herself with potassium cyanide. Efforts by Carrie Sterling to save her came too late. The suicide of the star-crossed, twenty-seven-year-old poet caused an uproar in the press and among the artists and writers at Carmel. It was common gossip on Ocean Avenue that the blond and gifted poet had become distraught over a hopeless entanglement with a married man. Yet the shock of Nora May French's death was deepened by the memory of her salty wit and her frequent talk of suicide. The memorial gathering at Point Lobos, to cast her cremated ashes to the winds, was a sad moment. While her former lovers glared at each other across the rocks, a fight broke out over who should throw the poet's ashes; and as Sterling, Hopper, and Lafler wrestled with each other on the ground, another member of the funeral party cast Nora May's remains into the sea.

In the months following Nora May French's death, a thick gray fog settled over the little redwood houses of the Carmelites as the inhabitants left the coast for other places. Mary Austin, convinced her death was near, had left for Rome, vowing to die in Italy. Her pilgrimage, however, did not end in tragedy.

Instead, apparently cured of cancer by spiritual disciples of the Blue Nuns and a simple vegetarian diet, Austin continued to produce innovative literature while she was abroad. The autobiographical *Earth Horizon* and *The Arrow-Maker*, a play using "Amerindian" rhythms, were launched in New York. *Lost Borders*, a companion piece to *Land of Little Rain*, introduced her to an admiring English public that included George Bernard Shaw and Joseph Conrad. But Mary Austin's greatest creative surge took place on her return to Carmel, when between 1911 and 1914, seven works were published in London and New York.

The suicide of Nora May French left deep scars on the psyche of George Sterling. In later years, after many of his old comrades had passed on, he never missed a sentimental pilgrimage to Point Lobos on the anniversary of her death. She was, in truth, his one unattainable golden beauty, for while she lived he did not touch her. Her passing seemed to suspend Sterling in a paralysis of despair, as if he were face-to-face with his own mortality. His maniacal drinking deteriorated into a serious alcoholic syndrome, relieved only briefly by fits of strenuous exercise and a diet of health foods. In 1909, his friend Charles Stoddard, the gentle bohemian, died peacefully at Monterey. His funeral, with Sterling as a pallbearer, was one more sad farewell. By the summer of 1911, the writer Van Wyck Brooks remarked that "George Sterling of Carmel-by-the-Sea had precisely the aspect of Dante in Hell."

Yet at the Bohemian Grove, Sterling was a respected and revered symbol of California's romantic past. When he attended costume parties then in vogue, he invariably dressed himself as a monk or pagan god. His morbid, alcoholic vision of suicide was but one more expression of his colorful and complex personality. His many friends responded to his charm and to his theatrical presence. For them, he was the archetypal poet, the torchbearer of a romantic tradition, curator of the Golden Age.

There is no wind to stir the cypress tree.
  Amber and chill the lucid sunset sank,
  A wine the breathless lips of Evening drank.
Peace is upon the headland and the sea.

The foam but whispers on the fading shore.
  Solemn and desolate the ocean lies,
  Azure of deeper twilight than the skies'
The night's enormous house is built once more.

The last dark gull has left the northern dune —
  So clear against the sky-line, though so far.
  A great, a calm, a slowly westering star
Goes down the heavens with a slender moon.

The shadows of eternity remain—
  The sense of wonder that the stars recall
  Here Beauty everlasting renders all—
Her sorrow that is joy, her holy pain.

— George Sterling, "After Sunset"

AT HOME IN CARMEL, offstage, George Sterling's relationship with his loyal wife crumbled in the aftermath of one too many infidelities. Amidst the beach-carnival of parties and visiting dignitaries and the loneliness, Carrie Sterling left Carmel for her sister's home in Berkeley. After a brief reconciliation, the separation became final. Carrie Sterling's subsequent abandonment of their marriage to divorce sent George into a deep depression. Long hikes down the south coast did not help, interspersed as they were with savage drinking, nor did the calming salve of friendship.

Jack London, after returning from an abortive two years in the Pacific, isolated himself in alcohol and drugs at his ranch in Sonoma. Ambrose Bierce, in a brief reunion with Sterling, decided that he had had enough of his former protégé's radicalism and open philandering and vowed to end the relationship for good. While Jimmy Hopper was in France, Sterling's old drinking partner Joaquin Miller died beside his self-erected funeral pyre in Oakland. George Sterling's noble experiment, his personal involvement with a colony of friends and fellow artists, was coming to an end. Even the return of Mary Austin and the founding of the Forest Theater at Carmel-by-the-Sea failed to lift his sense of loss.

January 1914 marked George Sterling's departure from the Carmel coast. Except for rare visits to the site of Nora May French's memorial place at Point Lobos, Sterling spent the rest of his life in the "cruel atmosphere" of cities — first in Greenwich Village and finally in San Francisco.

In his attempts to live in the shadow of classical antiquity, George Sterling was imprisoned by the very time boundaries he sought to transcend. By the time the philanthropist James Duval Phelan sent him money to return to San Francisco, his world had collapsed around him. First, Ambrose Bierce had disappeared in Mexico. And in 1916, his close friend Jack London died suddenly of an overdose of alcohol and drugs. Then came the shattering news of yet another suicide in California. Four years after her divorce, Carrie Sterling had put Chopin's funeral march on her gramophone and swallowed cyanide.

After Sterling's return to San Francisco, he occupied a third-floor room at the Bohemian Club, where, for the rest of his life, he was supported by rich men and women. Other than a brief tour in Hollywood, where he wrote subtitles for *The Thief of Bagdad*, the middle-aged Sterling stayed close to home. He contributed sporadically to local journals and occasionally wrote nostalgic pieces for H. L. Mencken's *American Mercury*. Publication of *Selected Poems* by a New York publisher brought only momentary satisfaction; as usual, the eastern critics had turned away from his archaic rhymes. The ravages of age and abuse lined his once-handsome face, and his continual excesses hospitalized him with alcoholic seizures and venereal disease.

When the body of George Sterling was discovered in his room at the Bohemian Club on November 17, 1926, it was apparent that he had finally used the cyanide he always carried with him. Cast about his room were the remains of recently burned papers and remnants of his poetry.

Deeper into the darkness I peer
Than most, yet find the darkness still beyond.

Before he died, George Sterling had the good fortune to know and to appreciate the early work of the great poet of the coast, Robinson Jeffers. In remembrance of his halcyon days in Carmel, Sterling passed the torch of poetry to the hands of genius.

Artist Colony

DURING THE FIRST DECADES of the new century, Carmel-by-the-Sea grew from a sparsely populated, bohemian settlement to an important and surprisingly productive community of artists, writers, poets, scientists, and academicians. Scattered within the colorful and homogeneous social fabric of Frank Devendorf's little enclave over the hill from the Del Monte were the summer homes of wealthy patrons. While George Sterling, Jack London, Jimmy Hopper, and other bohemians indulged themselves in dramas of wine and abalone, another quite different Carmel community was growing up around them. This stable, quieter group tolerated Sterling's antics and depression with the same good-natured neighborliness and laissez-faire that made town projects such as the annual Dutch Fair and Craft Show successful. Gossip circulated, as in all towns big or small, but the solid citizens of Carmel generally kept to themselves, observing what they called the "Barbary Coast" with some degree of humor.

As word of the Carmel community spread, more creative people were lured to the Monterey Coast from around the country. Of the new arrivals, the most famous was Upton Sinclair, who came to Carmel in 1908 after fire had gutted his Helicon Hall Home Colony, a writers' commune in New Jersey.

On the beach at Carmel, Sinclair let the bohemians know what he thought of their daydreaming, their lack of purpose and discipline, and their preoccupation with trivia. This coastal community was not, in his view, a fit companion for his utopian-socialist experiment in the East. He found it a hedonist's resort, and after three months among the Carmelites, Sinclair retreated to San Francisco.

When "Uppie" left Carmel, two sisters, both of whom shared avidly his social philosophy and had been fellow members of his commune at Helicon Hall, stayed on. In the legendary fire that destroyed the Home Colony, the sisters, writers Alice MacGowan and Grace MacGowan Cooke, saved themselves from the flames by jumping from a second-story window into the outstretched arms of the founder — an act of socialistic unity that spared the women's lives but put all three in the hospital. The MacGowan sisters later followed Uppie to Carmel, where they purchased a two-story home near what would be called Cooke's Cove. Their dedication to the politics of reform and writing left them little time to frolic on the beach with Sterling's crowd.

By the time they had settled into their routine, another Helicon youngster, Hal "Red" Lewis, arrived to spend the summer as secretary to the MacGowan sisters. The secretary was later to win the Nobel Prize for literature under his full name, Sinclair Lewis.

Sinclair Lewis at the Dutch Fair

Still the presence of George Sterling hovered over the Monterey Coast. The legendary poet laureate of Carmel had dared to fail; lost in the catacombs of vanity. The early Carmelites followed him and charmed themselves with a romance of seacoast and self-sufficiency, taking all from the coastal experience and giving little in return.

Others became victims of the furies of the coast. For beneath the dilettantism and honest creativity that characterized the artists' colony at Carmel-by-the-Sea lay a dark energy that was the undercurrent of the coastal experience. The endless parties at the beach, the constant talk of socialism and art for art's sake, and the vision of a romanticized theatrical death, had become ritual masks of ennui.

A summer of pale gold light and luminous shadows opened the senses to a euphoria of nature in counterpoint to rhythms of night breakers and cleansing sea fog. But away from community, humans were forced to contemplate the Ultimate Questions: Where did we come from? Why are we here? Where are we going?

Away from the beaches, coastal formations seemed placed in another time. Always, the overpowering, primal force of the ocean seemed poised to hurl itself toward land from a point just beyond an infinite horizon. To remind us that we are One.

IN THE SPRING OF 1910, a new community venture expanded the little theater movement that was gaining a following throughout the country. Founded by Herbert Heron Peet, a playwright from a theatrical family in Southern California, the Forest Theater was located on land occupying one city block southeast of Ocean Avenue. The property was initially leased to the Forest Theater Society by Frank Devendorf at no charge. After Heron (he had dropped the name Peet) had successfully launched fifteen years of summer productions, the developer sold the property to the theater for a modest two thousand dollars; in this way, Devendorf became the sponsor for a venture managed by local artists.

The natural amphitheater curved down like a Greek theater to an earthen floor covered with pine needles. The surrounding trees formed rough-hewn natural columns behind the players. Often during a performance, the fog would drift down over the tops of the forested set until the entire tableau assumed the character of an ancient Chinese scroll painting. The distant surf provided ambient sound for productions that ran the gamut from the Bible to Shakespeare.

During the years 1911-1914, the social life of Carmel-by-the-Sea revolved around the intramural feuds and creative bickering that accompanied each production of the Forest Theater Society. Carmel had become a town of over four hundred homes, three hotels, and Samuel F. B. Morse's newly constructed Del Monte Lodge in Pebble Beach. New arrivals to the artists' and writers' colony reflected the prestige and elegance of what was to become a highly fashionable and expensive leisure resort community.

Herbert Heron Peet

The Forest Theater

86

Mary Austin and cast of The Forest Theater

*If you think a glass factory is of greater importance than
a sand dune, or a millionaire than an artist,
a mansion than a little brown cottage.*

*If you truly want Carmel to become a boosting, hustling,
wideawake, lively metropolis,
Don't Vote for Perry Newberry*

— From a poster on the town bulletin board
Daisy Bostick and Dorothea Castelhun, *Carmel at Work and Play*

T HE EARLY 1900s saw the sleepy town of Carmel-by-the-Sea awakened by Samuel F. B. Morse's expansionist efforts with his Del Monte Forest, Cypress Point, and Pebble Beach resorts to the north. The Carmelites quickly united to incorporate their township in order to control further development, but there was disagreement over how best to save the town. Shopkeepers and the general business community wanted to promote Carmel's unique charm and resort potential to the outside world; conservationists and artists fought to keep Carmel the quiet seaside town it had always been.

Over the next thirteen years of bickering, the village of Carmel remained in the hands of the environmental cause and was served by two enlightened mayors, both former leading lights of the Forest Theater Society: founder Herbert Heron and Perry Newberry, a journalist and illustrator.

Although a planning commission was founded in 1922 to save Carmel from the evils of commerce, Ocean Avenue eventually became a paved thoroughfare lined with fashionable shops, and a highway was extended over the hill from Monterey. And by 1929, the fight between the artists' colony and the general community had become this country's first ecological advertising campaign. Perry Newberry ran for city trustee on the following platform: "Believing that what 9,999 towns out of 10,000 want is just what Carmel shouldn't have, I am a candidate for trustee on the platform, DON'T BOOST! I am making a spirited campaign to win by asking those who disagree to vote against me."

Newberry was elected. Immediately, a landmark zoning ordinance followed, wherein the residential character of Carmel took precedence over all future commercial development.

MANY OF CARMEL'S ARTISTS and writers did turn their creative talents toward real estate, community development, or politics. But a serious group of artists still vigorously pursued their work in the days following World War I. Perhaps the best-known artists of Carmel during the twenties and thirties were Armin Hansen, Charles Rollo Peters, William Ritschel, and Francis McComas, all of whom went on to international acclaim.

Of the four, Armin Hansen stands out as the leading influence on Carmel's artistic community. As an etcher, he was considered the greatest master since Whistler. Hansen, born in San Francisco in 1886, the son of watercolorist Hermann Wendleborg Hansen, was immediately drawn to the waterfront of Monterey. His evocative etchings won a gold medal in Paris and first prize in 1947 from the Chicago Society of Etchers. A spirited and fine teacher, Hansen became the Carmel Art Association's first president and a director for several years. He distinguished himself as an artist who harmoniously captured the spirit of life at sea.

While the wharves and ships were Hansen's first love, Charles Rollo Peters sensitively evoked the evening mystery of the coast. Master of the nocturne, Peters' brooding paintings of adobes nostalgically recall the life of bygone Monterey. Born in San Francisco in 1862, Peters traveled extensively for a number of years before returning home to marry Kathleen Mary Murphy. Peters worked tirelessly in his little studio near the couple's large estate overlooking Monterey Bay. Although small in stature, Peters was an imposing figure, standing before his easel dressed like a country squire.

Near Point Lobos, in a stone castle perched in the Carmel Highlands, lived another eminent artist, William Ritschel. The only American to have distinguished himself as a three-time winner of the acclaimed Ranger Prize from the National Acade-

my of Design, Ritschel had earned a significant reputation for his marine and landscape paintings. In Carmel, he could often be seen robed in an Oriental sarong, painting intensely at the edge of a cliff with his easel before him, staring first at his canvas and then out across the ocean.

William Ritschel

Considered by many as the greatest watercolorist of the West, Francis McComas ranked just behind Winslow Homer and John Marin. He was the only West Coast artist to have three works exhibited at the landmark Armory show of 1913. He arrived in Monterey in 1899 and moved to Pebble Beach, where he lived until his death in 1938. The McComases — Francis and his wife, Gene Baker, the talented artist and newspaper heiress — were prominent members of the artistic and social community of Pebble Beach and Del Monte Lodge. Rich with ultramarine blues, deep crimsons, and sun-washed yellows of the California hills, Francis McComas's murals enliven many Monterey public buildings, including the library, city council chambers, and the United States Naval Postgraduate School.

Samuel F. B. Morse, one of McComas' Pebble Beach neighbors, was his most supportive patron. Distinguished more by his creative talents in the area of resort development, Morse nonetheless had the artist's love and respect for the natural resources of Monterey, and with his theatrical bent, he also enjoyed the area as a dramatic backdrop for outrageous social affairs. The most famous soirée of the 1940s was his "Night in a Surrealist Forest," employing the talents of the leading master of surrealism, artist Salvador Dalí. For the party, Dalí requested that a menagerie of wild animals from the San Francisco Zoo be shipped down to roam Del Monte Forest. Dalí's only regret was that the zoo could not supply a giraffe. But giraffes notwithstanding, the event was a great success that is still recalled to this day. Herbert Cerwin, who helped stage the event, once remarked, "It is important to live in the right place at the right time, and in the late '30s and early '40s it was the Monterey Peninsula."

Salvador Dalí on the Monterey Peninsula

Photograph by Julian P. Graham, Pebble Beach HARRISON MEMORIAL LIBRARY

SAM MORSE'S CONCERN for the landscape was expressed most significantly in his relentless efforts to preserve the fragile natural resources of Pebble Beach. His foresight was responsible for saving 17 Mile Drive — the most spectacular stretch of coast in Monterey — from the builders and shopkeepers. An enlightened naturalist, Morse initiated a system of greenbelts, including a series of golf courses that today continue to draw thousands of professional and amateur golfers from around the world. His sharply restricted building code in Del Monte Forest has preserved the great pine woods sighted by Vizcaíno nearly four hundred years ago. The only commercial enterprises included Del Monte Lodge and a small sand-mining operation, no longer in use.

In the late 1930s, a small private school was established above the lodge on Forest Lake Road in Del Monte Forest. A "finishing school" for young ladies, with emphasis on manners and horsemanship the school was run by a strong matriarch, Grace Parsons Douglas, who gave her name to the school. She was assisted in the school's management by Dick Collins, who ran the horseback riding program and who was eventually to develop the equestrian center, now as important to Pebble Beach life as the area's golf courses.

The school, under increasing competition from the Santa Catalina School in nearby Monterey, was sold in 1952 to Robert U. Ricklefs, a respected educator and retired army officer who had served on Eisenhower's staff. Real estate values in the Forest were quite depressed at the time, and the founders were able to acquire the property at a bargain price. The three original investors were: Ricklefs; John Lyon Reid, an architect whose Chapel design was to bring national recognition to the school in 1964; and S. Fletcher Dutton, a retired Spreckels Sugar executive.

From their shoestring investment, this school, named for Robert Louis Stevenson, has grown to a coeducational enrollment of more than four hundred fifty day and boarding students. With its high academic standards, it ranks with the country's finest preparatory schools, and its fifty acres of pine forest are now graced with olympic-class sports facilities, modern academic buildings, and dormitories, as well as with the beautiful Keck Auditorium, where the school provides a regular series of musical, dramatic, and forensic performances for residents of the Monterey Peninsula.

While the Del Monte Forest development flourished, businessmen on the Monterey Peninsula were challenged with the choice of protecting or "developing" the land itself. Ultimately, concerns for human ecology turned the imagination inward, challenging artists, writers, and scientists to recreate the spirituality and grandeur that is the essence of the coastal experience.

An effort to understand the mysteries of natural sea life had long been under way just north of Del Monte Forest on an exposed rocky headland called "China Point" by the locals. Since 1892, when Hopkins Marine Station was founded as the first marine laboratory on the Pacific Coast, environmental scientists have established new standards of excellence in the field of marine biology. Located on one of the world's unique intertidal shorelines, Hopkins Marine Station, a branch of Stanford University, has continued to attract graduate students and eminent research biologists. Today, brilliantly colored starfish, sea anemones, and microscopic organisms, as well as seals and fish, are protected by a marine reserve that surrounds the mile-long waterfront of the station. Nearby, on Cannery Row, the Monterey Bay Aquarium, financed by the David Packard family, is a dramatic public showcase for the marine life of the Monterey Coast.

The Pebble Beach Golf Links

92

Masters of the Coast

*I*T HAS BEEN SAID THAT when he was twenty-seven, the great poet of the Monterey Coast, Robinson Jeffers, and his new wife, Una, came upon George Sterling's place of meditation while exploring the pine forests above Carmel. The austerity of the tall trees, grouped in silence around natural stones, suggested an ancient druidic ruin. For Jeffers, this mystical land and luminous coastal tableau held a vision that would inspire his life's work.

Two other great artists, John Steinbeck, who was a generation younger than Jeffers, and the photographer Edward Weston, shared in the quest for an art that reflected the inner rhythms of the coast. Steinbeck, in his major novels *Cannery Row, East of Eden,* and *The Grapes of Wrath*, displayed such humanism and mastery of prose style that he was accorded, in 1972, the Nobel Prize for literature. Edward Weston, with his dynamic sense of form in nature and his virtuosity in printing, introduced black-and-white photography as one of the major arts of the twentieth century. In the timeless compositions of Edward Weston, the modern verse of Jeffers, and the humanistic novels of Steinbeck, a great art was finally fashioned from the coastal iconography that had consumed George Sterling. This new art broke through the barriers of regionalism and popular romanticism into the mainstream of the modern cultural movement. The fresh vision of Jeffers, Steinbeck, and Weston focused the attention of international modernists on the Monterey Coast.

Robinson Jeffers and George Sterling
MONTEREY PUBLIC LIBRARY

If you should look for this place after a handful of lifetimes:
Perhaps of my planted forest a few
May stand yet, dark-leaved Australians or the coast cypress, haggard
With storm-drift; but fire and the axe are devils.
Look for foundations of sea-worn granite, my fingers had the art
To make stone love stone, you will find some remnant.
But if you should look in your idleness after ten thousand years:
It is the granite knoll on the granite
And lava tongue in the midst of the bay, by the mouth of the Carmel
River-valley, these four will remain
In the change of names. You will know it by the wild sea-fragrance of the wind
Though the ocean may have climbed or retired a little;
You will know it by the valley inland that our sun and our moon were born from
Before the poles changed; and Orion in December
Evenings was strung in the throat of the valley like a lamp-lighted bridge.
Come in the morning you will see white gulls
Weaving a dance over the blue water, the wane of the moon
Their dance-companion, a ghost walking
By daylight, but wider and whiter than any bird in the world.
My ghost you needn't look for; it is probably
Here, but a dark one, deep in the granite, not dancing on wind
With the mad wings of the day moon.

— Robinson Jeffers, "Tor House"

94

ROBINSON JEFFERS WAS BORN IN 1887 in Pittsburgh, Pennsylvania, to a privileged family. His father, a reserved Presbyterian theology professor, had married Jeffers' strikingly beautiful mother late in life. By the age of fifteen, their only child had read avidly the great works of classical literature. After private schooling in Europe and on the East Coast, Jeffers moved with his family to Pasadena, where he graduated from Occidental College at eighteen. He went on to advanced studies in languages, forestry, and medical science at the University of Southern California.

While in Southern California, Jeffers met his future wife, Una Call Kuster, who was then married to another man. The meeting embroiled him in a despairing, tempestuous courtship that lasted almost eight years. Although Jeffers was highly educated and might well have become an academic scholar, he always knew that he would become a poet. His early writing, of the Los Angeles period, showed little sign of genius, since his love affair dissipated his energies. But the storm in Robinson Jeffers' young life eventually lifted, and the two lovers finally ventured to the Monterey Coast as man and wife.

At the time of his marriage, Jeffers received an inheritance that supported his work and family for the rest of his life. Though the young couple first thought of leaving for Ireland, the onset of the Great War turned them to a site on Carmel Point. On this rocky promontory, Jeffers began to build Tor House, a stone building made of indigenous materials that had been softened by the sea. In this beautiful hand-built studio, Jeffers expressed the spirit of isolation and self-sufficiency that would guide the rest of his life. At Tor House, he confronted the elemental furies of nature and the undercurrents of his own dark spirit.

In 1924, Jeffers' first narrative poem, *Tamar*, became a literary sensation. Suddenly, at thirty-seven, the master of Tor House was being hailed as an important new voice on the American scene.

His earlier idealism, with its connection to the modern American transcendentalist movement, had disappeared with his first mature work. It was as if his youthful concern for man had been obliterated by the Great War of 1918. From his rocky vigil on the California coast, Jeffers turned away from the horror and the hopes of civilization to forge a new doctrine, a prophecy grounded in what the poet called "inhumanism."

> *I believe this hurt will be healed*
> *Some age of time after mankind has died.*

Almost immediately, the inhumanist doctrines of Robinson Jeffers enveloped him in a storm of controversy and criticism that lasted beyond his death. He had strengthened himself in the knowledge of the natural laws and in classical Greek literature. Unlike his predecessor George Sterling, who could not realize his vision, Jeffers was able to hold these two seemingly dissimilar influences within the delicate balance of an original art.

During the Depression years, Jeffers' career reached its zenith. The crash of sea that hollowed out great sentinel rocks at Point Sur echoed in the inhumanism and grandeur of the poet's blank verse. Just as Robinson Jeffers expressed his rage at humanity by ignoring the human being, he found his relentless spirit at one with the circling hawk or ancient natural stones worn by the furies of the sea. At times, his words were like the reverberations of some prehistoric earth-gong echoing out across a limitless space.

After the initial blast of *Tamar*, Jeffers attacked humanity's demons and obsessions. *Roan Stallion* and *The Woman at Point Sur*, Jeffers' later narrative poems, achieved his stated purpose to "strip everything but its natural ugliness from the unmorality." Then followed the great, long, dramatic narrative *Cawdor*, set on the Monterey Coast and considered by many to be his masterpiece of the period before World War II. In this work, doctrine was transcended by the story of the old rancher Cawdor, of his suffering and guilt, of the widower's tragic marriage to a sensuous young woman. In later works, Jeffers increased the intensity of his humanless space until it became filled with incantations to a universal God as the very image of natural law and beauty. Always, the incandescence of his words, the harsh realism of the sea, the timelessness of the south coast, evoked an even larger view of universe.

Robinson Jeffers' work, taken in total, begins to lead us to a new age of environmentalism — of reverence for natural law and for the land itself. During the 1940s, when Jeffers crafted his famous adaptation of Euripides' *Medea* for the great Greek tragedienne Judith Anderson, the world from which he had turned in horror erupted into another world war. There was no place to hide. Jeffers' doctrines began to fall from favor. His questioning of science and human survival in the postwar era left Jeffers virtually alone on his storm-swept coast.

The poet William Everson sees Jeffers as a prophet of "the stratosphere looking back at the earth from the blackness of outer space." Everson points up Jeffers' relevancy to new generations:

An economy of affluence and a mangling Viet Nam War have conspired to prepare an atmosphere of disenchantment and risk not unlike the mood in which Jeffers himself had quickened. Perhaps a new generation, sick of the suburbs, is finding his Big Sur isolation and his westering gaze as universal in their implication as an intermediate generation found them irrelevant.

Tor House built by Robinson Jeffers

Photograph by Julian P. Graham, Pebble Beach HARRISON MEMORIAL LIBRARY

THE MULTIMILLION-DOLLAR sardine bonanza that created Cannery Row on the bay near Monterey's old Custom House began in 1900 with Frank Booth's wood frame salmon-packing operation on Alvarado Street. Booth worked diligently, canning salmon by hand and saving his money, until a new species of sardine was observed swimming in dense, silvery schools under the piers of the Monterey waterfront. Soon Booth was canning the tiny fish, which seemed to frequent the bay in ever-increasing numbers. Before long, the cannery had moved to the back room of a saloon near the wharf; but in spite of his hard work, Booth could not deal with the abundant catch, so he again moved to larger quarters.

A young Norwegian icthyologist named Knute Hovden, graduate of the National Fisheries College in Oslo, then signed on to help solve Booth's dilemma by increasing the productivity and storage capacity of the sardine factory.

Soon afterward, the *lámpara* (lightning) net was introduced to Monterey by the Italian immigrant fisherman Pietro Ferrante. This net revolutionized the task of hauling masses of sardines from the waters. With the new net, fishermen could move in to catch large quantities of the little fish in split-second time. Thus, when war in Europe abruptly cut off the supply of fish from Mediterranean waters, the canning industry on Monterey Bay boomed. By 1918, the new assembly-line techniques improved productivity until twenty-seven canneries were operating on what became known as Cannery Row. Eventually, the little port of Monterey held a third-place position among world producers of fish.

Ferrante attained prestige and success in his adopted country as a leader of the immigrant colony of Italian-American fishermen and by establishing Monterey's powerful Fishermen's Union and Boat Owners' Association. But, in the years following World War II, the annual catch leveled off until the sardine fell victim to the same overfishing that had depleted the whaling industry during the 1870s.

One of the side effects of the Great Depression and the turmoil that accompanied the growth of the fishing-and-canning industry along Cannery Row was the existence of a colorful, waterfront slum society. This world was brought to life by a new American novelist, John Steinbeck, when the now-classic *Cannery Row* was published in 1945. In this masterwork, Steinbeck fashioned a profoundly human drama about the people who squatted in tenements near the canneries. His characters included a Chinese shopkeeper, Yee Won; the whores of Flora Wood's Lone Star Cafe; the bum-hero; scavengers of the waterfront; and "Doc" Ricketts, a real-life marine biologist and philosopher-in-residence during the Depression.

Cannery Row Fishermen
MONTEREY PUBLIC LIBRARY

98

Steinbeck's earlier masterworks — *Tortilla Flat, Of Mice and Men*, and *The Grapes of Wrath*, which was made into a movie by John Ford — had established his international reputation as a populist reformer and as the premier novelist of rural California. His humanist concerns and his genius for dialogue, in what he called his conversational style, established his novels as bestsellers of the Depression years. A native son of the Salinas Valley, he took his material from contemporary experience of the 1930s and created works of art that transcended his times. A biblical scholar and master of a deceptively simple writing style, he brought to the land about which he wrote another kind of recognition — the Nobel Prize for literature.

Steinbeck was born in Salinas of a German-Irish family. Both his father, a county treasurer, and his mother encouraged him in his development as a writer. After early years at Stanford University as an English-journalism major, the young Steinbeck, always working at labor jobs, began to turn out a strongly original prose, modern in style but biblical in influence. His early successes led to many other powerful works, among them *East of Eden* and *The Log from the Sea of Cortez*, written with his friend Edward F. "Doc" Ricketts. Throughout his career, Steinbeck's identification with the land and his love for the untouched beauty of old California — the "Long Valley" that lay between the Gabilan and Santa Lucia mountain ranges — brought out his most consistently brilliant and sensitive writing.

In Steinbeck's vision, the rewards of simple living and of environmental morality far exceeded those of the material world. In his best works, the traditions of old California were extended into the mainstream of American letters. As he wrote in *Travels with Charley*, published in 1962:

The Pacific is my home ocean; I knew it first, grew up on its shore, collected marine animals along the coast. I know its moods, its color, its nature. It was very far inland that I caught the first smell of the Pacific. When one has been long at sea, the smell of land reaches far out to greet one. And the same is true when one has been long inland. I believe I smelled the rocks and the kelp and the excitement of churning sea water, the sharpness of iodine and the under odor of washed and ground calcareous shells. Such a far-off and remembered odor comes subtly so that one does not consciously smell it but rather an electric excitement is released — a kind of boisterous joy — I discovered long ago in collecting and classifying marine animals that what I found was closely intermeshed with how I felt at the moment.

John Steinbeck

Photo Portrait of Edward Weston

Photograph by William Heick

A THIRD ARTIST, EDWARD WESTON, arrived from Southern California to establish a studio in Carmel. To the science of photography, Weston brought new insights and a powerful vision. In Weston's photographs the coastal experience is expressed with both truth and universality of form.

Weston was a native of Illinois, born in 1886. By 1919, he had married, fathered four sons, and was ensconced in a studio in Southern California. His earlier work in portraiture and figurative composition, echoing the influence of Japanese art and James McNeill Whistler, had won prizes, numerous one-man exhibitions, and commercial success. He was elected to the official London Salon and seemed destined to pursue a stylistic formula based on a highly theatrical use of tonality and pictorial representation.

Then, doubtlessly influenced by avant-garde art at the 1915 Panama-Pacific Exposition, Weston began to dissociate himself from the establishment and to experiment with abstract compositions based on an innovative use of light. Further exposure to the New York modernist school of Alfred Stieglitz and Paul Strand and to the precisionist paintings and photographs of Charles Sheeler brought him firmly into the mainstream of the modern art movement of the 1920s.

After translating the Ohio Armco Steel Works into stark, vertical lines that anticipated high technology and industrial architecture of the international style, Weston's photography began to center on form itself. In his first experiments, fragments of his subjects appeared to be juxtaposed with large, flat, triangular planes and forms of interior space. Now, Weston began to examine the fragments themselves, in close-up.

Again, the stimulus of travel, inspired by his Mexican apprentice, Tina Modotti, provided the photographer with both subject and ambiance to break through the fashionable, soft-focus salon style of the period. The harsh light of Mexico, the vitality of Mexican mural art, and the cross-fertilization and exchange of ideas with such Mexican masters as José Clemente Orozco and Diego Rivera nurtured Weston's work. As his camera moved toward his subject, the form became monumental, a composition within itself, and the distribution of the natural light over images became critical. He concentrated on close studies of shells, vegetables, and fragments of the female form, nearly always without emphasis on the head or "personality" of the subject. In the great still lifes of his middle period, Weston was preparing for an integration of essential form with nature. This near-impossible synthesis was finally achieved in the major works created around Weston's famous studio near Wildcat Creek in the Carmel Highlands.

Beginning with the major works of the 1930s, Weston's long and productive Carmel period brought the photographer international recognition. Gone were the tentative experiments in abstraction of the 1920s and the strong but pictorial compositions inspired by the Mexican experience. Closer studies of natural forms, such as peppers and sea shells, evoked a powerful emotional response to what were deceptively symmetrical compositions. The mysterious light and tone of the shells brought forth an interior illumination that radiated a curious sensuality from the surface of the photograph. The Weston genius for conceptualization and realization of form-in-nature emerged in the reality of a bold, new study in monumentality, *Driftwood Stump* (1937). The sheer power of this work suggests the interchangability of the human image and nature.

The study of form was soon integrated into works exploring the larger and more complex reality of the inspiring seacoast.

Compositional relationships were dynamic, always in motion, unlike the minimal black space of the still lifes or the gray tone that brought the driftwood cypress trunk into forced close-up. In masterpieces of the Carmel period, Weston confounded time and perpetual motion, bringing in an instant the coastal image beyond the world of painters and poets into the purely black-and-white terms of photography. Finally, the deep-focus, hard-edged reality of the mature Weston style was intensified by the natural luminosity of the forms and highlights of the coast.

In the middle of the Great Depression, Weston received funding from the government-sponsored Public Works of Art Project. Three years later, he received the first Guggenheim Foundation Fellowship awarded to a photographer for a series on the American West. These fortuitous commissions enabled Weston to proceed with his photography, uninterrupted by the economic turmoil of the times, and to establish himself permanently in his famed studio-home on the Monterey Coast. From this small retreat, built in 1938 by his son Niel, the photographer completed his final work.

After publication of *California and the West*, with a text by Charis Wilson, who had accompanied him on his Guggenheim-funded journey, and major representation in the Limited Editions Club, for which he illustrated Walt Whitman's *Leaves of Grass*, Weston turned again to his old coastal haunts. Masterworks of this period after the war were executed while Weston was suffering the long and painful trauma of Parkinson's Disease. In these works, the exquisite rhythms and forms of the cypress forests at Point Lobos found a new order. Weston's black-and-white technique evoked an essence of the coastal image — the sentinel rock, the pine forests, and the cypresses. Weston had waited for the exact moment before releasing his shutter, in order to unify the intricate patterns that played before him on the ground glass of the camera. The delicate accents of illumination on the bare ghost-trunks of the cypress trees revealed their relationship, in what seems a primordial time, to the natural arrangement of rocks and shadows below them. The lone cypress appeared to hover over the presence of the great snags of its sister trees like some ancient shrine to nature.

Although time was running out for Edward Weston, in the refinement and classical balance of *Point Lobos*, he created a world of infinite theme and variation, recalling the music of Bach. From one point of view, the more traditional relationships of space and form were composed on triangular lines of movement from a foreground of emerging rocks and boulders into deeper horizontal lines of cypress foliage. From another standpoint, forms that had been selected by the photographer appeared to be dominated by a floating, surface tension in the manner of ancient Chinese painting.

In the simplicity of his black-and-white photography, Weston presents us with not only a reconciliation of science and art, but also with the inevitable fusion of Eastern and Western concepts as inspired by nature. Like Steinbeck and Jeffers, Weston illuminated the essence and spirit of the coastal experience for those who were to come.

Big Sur and the Oranges of Henry Miller

Artists never thrive in colonies. Ants do.
— Henry Miller, *Big Sur and the Oranges of Hieronymus Bosch*

THE EARLY DEVELOPMENT of the coastal land south of the Carmel River along the western slope of the Santa Lucia Mountains occurred gradually, beginning in the mid-nineteenth century. Much of this seventy-mile strip of inaccessible redwood wilderness and plunging cliffs remained unscathed by civilization until the onset of World War II. Only with the completion of Highway 1 in June 1937 did the breathtaking panorama of the south coast become known to tourists and pilgrims in search of an American paradise. To artists, writers, poets, philosophers, and seers, the south coast became the ultimate retreat, a place of relentless silence above the sea.

The splendid isolation of its forests and the stark grandeur of its Pacific vistas opened human sensibilities to an immediate and all-pervasive confrontation with nature. The American writer Henry Miller, who lived on Partington Ridge in Big Sur, stated: "If the soul were to choose an arena in which to stage its agonies, this would be the place for it. One feels exposed — not only to the elements, but to the sight of God."

Henry Miller
HENDERSON COLLECTION

Large parcels of the rugged, inhospitable terrain had been divided up by the traditional Mexican land-grant method. Rancho El Sur, the nine thousand-acre grant south along the Little Sur River, was ceded to Juan Bautista Alvarado, and Rancho San José y Sur Chiquita, located in the northernmost area of Big Sur, to Teodoro Gonzales. Neither hijo del país established an adobe on his remote land. Five years later, Alvarado, acting in his new capacity as governor, regranted Rancho San José to Marcelino Escobar, extending the territory "inland as far as the cattle graze." Don Marcelino promptly lost his magnificent wilderness domain in a dice game to his friend David Castro, who eventually sold out to the Americans.

Alvarado soon liquidated his El Sur estate in favor of his uncle, Juan Bautista Roger Cooper, who opened the land to cattle ranching. The Cooper ranch later passed down through relatives under the stewardship of Andrew Molera, the legendary rancher and jack cheese maker, whose family donated the original grant in Big Sur to the Nature Conservancy, which sold it to the state of California for park use. It is known today as the Molera Ranch and State Park.

After the annexation of California by the United States, the remaining acreage of the south coast was opened to homesteading by a process called preemption, whereby 160-acre parcels were offered to settlers at $1.25 per acre. In 1853, George Davis of Monterey became the first American to build a small cabin in Redwood Valley, close to the Big Sur River. Davis did little with his claim and sold his cabin to Emmanuel Innocenti and his family for fifty dollars. Innocenti, an educated Native convert from Mission Santa Barbara and a former head vaquero at the Cooper ranch, devoted his life to farming the fertile valley land near what was later called Mount Manuel at present-day Pfeiffer-Big Sur State Park.

The Homestead Act of 1862, passed by Congress with Abraham Lincoln's signature during the Civil War, opened more of the south coast to settlement. William Brainard Post, a foreman at Rancho San José y Sur Chiquita, became one of the first founding fathers of Big Sur. The first post office and schoolhouse were located at his ranch near what became known as the Post Grade, and later the combined family homestead was expanded to include almost nineteen hundred acres. Other rugged, good-hearted pioneer families homesteaded the Big Sur country, as drought in the Salinas Valley brought settlers westward over the Santa Lucias to the fog-bound slopes of the Pacific. From these hardy men and women, the creeks and canyons of the south coast were to derive their names. Partington, Trotter, Grimes, Torre, Bixby, Notley — all left their imprint on the land, along with Slate, Anderson, Dolan, Walter, Harlan, Dani, McWay, and the young Borondas.

The early Big Sur community united around a pioneer family named Pfeiffer, who brought to the south coast a respect for the land that reflected the simple traditions of an earlier era in old California. These first settlers of the wilderness coast radiated the same vitality and sense of hospitality that made dolce far niente a unique experience in the American West. Yet in their boisterous struggle for self-sufficiency, the early families had little time for long days of sweet idleness.

To the north of Big Sur, the old rancheros of Cooper and Soberanes raised cattle on the grassy meadows of the Pacific slope. In Sycamore Valley, the Pfeiffers and their friendly neighbors, the Innocentis, hunted and farmed the land until it provided fair sustenance for their families. The early days were full and bright, and it became a family ritual for Michael Pfeiffer, his young wife, Barbara, and their little sons to labor together beneath the sun-speckled trees near their log house at Bears-Kill-Two-Calves Creek. But the struggle of dawn-to-dusk farming was never quite enough to keep the Pfeiffer larder full. When money was needed for flour, sugar, and other staples, Barbara Pfeiffer supervised the work of the homestead, while her husband worked for wages as a farmhand in Salinas.

On the ranches, the puma and the grizzly bear menaced the young families of Big Sur, killing colts, sheep, and cattle. The landlocked and remote canyons, the forested mountains, and the rugged wagon trails south to Point Sur created a haven for the giant bears, who killed the ranchers' stock almost at will. Soon the great predators grew so bold that they attacked their prey in open daylight, bashing in a steer's ribs with one huge paw, then tearing open the carcass to eat the fat from the stomach. The grizzlies might well have ended cattle ranching on the south coast had not Michael Pfeiffer poisoned the dreaded beasts with strychnine. Pfeiffer discovered that if he hung poisoned balls of steer fat in trees, above the reach of dogs, the hungry bears would always return to gorge themselves at the scene of the kill. Unfortunately, this battle for survival at Big Sur and elsewhere resulted in extinction of the California grizzly.

Post's Station

THE FOUNDING FAMILIES — the Castros, Pfeiffers, Partingtons, Innocentis, Posts, and other hardy settlers of the coast — shared a fellowship that was a joyous liberation from the hard loneliness of pioneer ranch life. Although the wagon trails were brutally steep and dangerous, families trekked for days on horseback and mule to celebrate a roof-raising or a fence-building with barbecues and dancing at a neighbor's ranch. These cooperative gatherings, where work assumed a higher purpose than daily toil, became more than social events. In a profound way, these good times were an extension of the best days of old California. The women exchanged food, preserves, honey, hams, and fresh baked bread and talked about their children and their new vision of life and freedom on the coast. Lillian Boss Ross' Big Sur novels describe with eloquence and nostalgia the harvest feasts, the weddings, and the impromptu dances:

Bill got his fiddle, Avery took his place and tweedled his flute while Henry came over with the accordion looking proud and sure of himself as he calls out, "The jota, Maria?"

Tony and Maria grabbed hands and run to the center as Henry turns to the other players and says, " 'Seville Lady,' that's the best tune."

It was something to see, something to hear, when that accordion turned loose on a dance tune. It made so much music a fellow had to listen careful to hear the fiddle and even the sharp flute couldn't come out to top it. The dance matched the music. I'd never saw Maria so light-footed, seen her teeth shine so steady as they did while the whole Coast watched her and her new husband do brand-new steps to the old jota. Tony tore off his red neckerchief and stomped around Maria, waving it like them bullfighters the Spanish like to tell tales of. Maria circled him like a fox circles a trap, but her face, her hands, all of her, coaxed him to catch her. Even while I was looking at it I was thinking I'd still see, still hear this music and dancing when I was old as Pa.

No one wanted them to stop. The hands clapping together drowned out the slap of the sea again' the cliffs and here and there was shouts of "More! More!"

— Lillian Boss Ross, *The Stranger*

In spite of the joy and stark beauty of this simple rural pageantry, it was inevitable that the more educated and ambitious pioneers would look for commercial means to improve the harsh living conditions of the times. The first venture, that of the engineer John Partington and Sam Trotter, was the development of a seacoast landing site from which to transport local tanbark and lumber products to ships offshore. Tanbark, which contains tannic acid, and rough, freshly cut redwood planking were soon to become the items of a thriving business in Sur country. Later, a competitor established Notley's Landing, which became both the site of one of the wildest dance halls on the coast and a rendezvous for smugglers and rumrunners during the days of Prohibition.

With the gradual improvement of the still-tortuous inland wagon trails, other business left its mark on the land. True to the mystique of early California, gold was discovered in the high mountains southeast of Pacific Valley. By late 1887, prospectors flocked to the area, opening small claims near W.D. Cruickshank's first discovery at "Last Chance." Other mines became briefly productive at Los Burros, Calizona, Gorda, and Melville until a veritable boomtown flourished in the godforsaken and inaccessible wilderness of the Santa Lucias. Like the Sierra encampments thirty years earlier, the town of Manchester soon sported a restaurant, five saloons, a dance hall, a butcher shop, two general stores, a confectionary, and a small hotel. Still, the remote and often impassable terrain of Los Burros Mining District could not support these miners in the manner of the gold fields of El Dorado or the silver mines of Nevada. In less than a decade, the town's three stamp mills stood silent and its buildings were abandoned to the elements.

Down the slope at Bixby Canyon, limestone mining was undertaken, and a company from Monterey constructed an elaborate aerial tramway system to the water, where lime was lowered in huge buckets to waiting ships. For nearly four years, mining operations bustled about the area known as Bixby Creek. But soon the best lime deposits were depleted, and when constant washouts and lack of firewood made the great kilns and tramways too expensive to operate, the small mining community became a ghost town overnight.

With the closing of the last mines in the Santa Lucia mountain range, commerce on the south coast depended on the imagination of the settlers. After many shipwrecks off the coast of Point Sur, a beautiful light house was constructed. Its lamp, designed in France, was installed in the tower four hundred feet above the Pacific, serving as both a warning to mariners and a symbol of pride for the Big Sur ranch hands who built it.

Meanwhile, Florence Pfeiffer, one of Michael Pfeiffer's daughters-in-law, began an enterprise that heralded a new era of rustic resort development of the valley land around the Big Sur River. She soon found herself with long-term tenants, who leased property across the river for private family campgrounds. Along the trail at Little Sur, a hotel advertised a full limit of trout to outdoorsmen who braved the ten-hour stagecoach trip down the coast from Monterey. Florence Pfeiffer's success caused others on the coast to offer accommodations to paying guests. Before long, outsiders from California cities began to eye the scenic wonders of Big Sur country for its material value as real estate. Huge sums of money — almost a quarter of a million dollars — were offered to John and Florence Pfeiffer for their holdings. It is a tribute to the morality of the founding families that many of them refused private sale and donated ranch lands and large ocean-front acreages for use as state parks. In this way, the soft beauty of the south coast was preserved for future generations.

Bixby Bridge under Contruction

WITH THE ADVENT of America's entrance into World War I, a state senator pushed through a highway bill as a "military necessity" for the defense of California and the nation. The engineering feat that became the Carmel-San Simeon Highway took eighteen years and ten million dollars to complete. By the time the first contracts were let in 1919, many of the original landowners had organized to fight new zoning regulations.

The grandeur of Big Sur and the solitude of its redwood rivers might have remained hidden from the world had not the spectacular Highway 1 been carved into the cliffs overhanging the Pacific Ocean along the Santa Lucia mountain range. This monumental task, requiring physical courage, great engineering skill, and enormous sums of taxpayers' money, resulted in more than one hundred miles of road from Carmel Highlands to San Simeon. The new paved highway replaced the Big Sur Stage and the narrow, winding trailway to Post's. By fall 1937, the first automobiles moved south toward Los Angeles.

The major construction of the road was accomplished by road gangs and convicts during the worst times of the Great Depression. Camps were set up at Little Sur and Kirk Creek, and two hundred convicts were encamped at the meadow overlooking Anderson Creek. The men worked with each other in good cheer, for jobs were hard to come by in those days. Labor gangs were often roped together on sheer cliff walls or hung from baskets to drill holes for dynamite blasting. Thirty-three bridges, including Bixby Bridge, then the longest concrete nonsuspension bridge in the world, were completed with but one tragic accident.

Somehow, the building of Bixby Bridge, spanning one of the deepest canyons of the Santa Lucias, symbolized the flight of people with creative sensibilities from the growing commercialism of Carmel and the Monterey Peninsula. The ascetic and often mysterious ambiance of Big Sur, the great silences in the redwoods, and the untouched primordial spaces cried out to the artists, the poets, and the philosophers.

The completion of Highway 1 and the dramatic crash and rescue of the giant United States Navy dirigible *Macon* off the coast of Point Sur were but a prelude to the conflagration that pulled America out of the Great Depression. The onset of World War II in Europe soon immersed the country, and the Monterey Peninsula, in wartime industry. Military training bases suddenly flourished on the sand dunes of Fort Ord, north of Monterey, bringing a cross section of the nation's youth into contact with the rarified and still-idyllic life-style of Carmel and Pebble Beach. The Hotel Del Monte, rebuilt in 1925 after another fire, had become the United States Naval Postgraduate School, and the shoreline of Monterey Bay was seen, once more, as the nation's first line of defense.

Labor Camp at Big Sur

LEGEND HAS IT that it was Jean Varda, the master collagist and colorist, who first introduced Henry Miller to the place that he would claim as paradise. Born in Brooklyn, Miller escaped to the expatriate life of Paris during the 1930s — following a tradition shared by Ernest Hemingway and F. Scott Fitzgerald. In the company of his second wife, June, and other writers and artists, including Anais Nin and the surrealist poet Antonin Artaud, Miller soon became the foremost spirit of this bohemian group. Although virtually unknown and unpublished at the time, Miller had already earned a reputation for his sexually explicit and otherwise avant-garde writing, which outraged conventional sensibilities at home and abroad. His lust for life and its endless bounty — hearty food, spirited women, and warm camaraderie — were expressed in his essays and novels and in his more autobiographical works, such as *The Colossus of Maroussi*, celebrating the exuberant life and people of Greece. In 1942, Henry Miller had just completed what he termed his "air-conditioned nightmare" trip around America, after first having been forced by the war from his writer's haven in the Greek Islands. By summer, he had "arrived in California to stay," venturing up the coast from Beverly Glen to visit in Big Sur and stay on as a permanent resident of Partington Ridge.

Certainly, it was more than war in Europe that brought the author of such classics as *Tropic of Cancer* and *The Rosy Crucifixion* to discover a new way of life on the south coast of California. In the beginning, Henry Miller's circle of literary and intellectual friends gathered together in simple communion at informal dinners or soirées at Slate's Hot Springs, much in the manner of the early pioneer ranchers. Their conversation was perhaps more rarefied, since their lives were concerned more with the celebration of the spirit than with the struggle with the land.

Miller pursued a frugal existence and held to a rigid schedule, writing in the early morning at his studio-home on Partington Ridge. Among the strong and gentle people who, like Miller, were able to live with the silence and loneliness of the coast were the novelist Lillian Boss Ross, her husband Harrydick Ross, the sculptor, and Jaime de Angulo, linguist, physician, anthropologist, and ethnologist. Later, the English nature poet Eric Barker and other artist-friends, including the painter Ephraim Doner, joined the Miller circle. In *My Bike and Other Friends*, Miller wrote of Doner:

> He is absolutely unique, undiluted, integral. One would like to write about him in Polish or Old French. English is too dull, too flat, too weak, to render his nature, his soul.... Chassidic as he is, he is always whirling about you, snapping his fingers and muttering prayers. He makes one dizzy immediately. Dizzy, thirsty and talkative. For he is an electrifier!...He went to his studio religiously every day — like a priest to mass...Without soul, a painting, like an individual, was to him dead.

This group of individualists united in friendship and a personal sense of self-reliance that made the Big Sur community different from the pretentious colony at Carmel-by-the-Sea. With Henry Miller's presence on Partington Ridge, a finer, more humane, and softening influence was sensed along the coast. Younger people, who read his work as the gospel of a new way of life apart from the "air-conditioned nightmare," were inspired by his commitment to what he called "the wisdom of the heart":

> I know there are some who complain that Big Sur does not offer enough stimulus. My feeling, on the contrary, is that there is too much stimulus. To the man whose senses are alive and alert there is not even the need to stir from one's threshold. For such a one there is a world here as full and rich, as completing and instructive, as Thoreau found at Walden.
>
> As a man who is in love with the world — the alien world — I must confess that I am also in love with my home, the first real home I have known. Doubtless those who appreciate "home" most are the eternal vagabonds, the outlaws. If I am ever to venture forth into the world again I trust I can now offer something of root as well as flower. To offer simply what Big Sur has taught me would be no small thing. I say Big Sur, not America. For however much a part of America Big Sur may be, and it is American through and through, what distinguishes it is something more than the word American conveys. If I were to single out an element in American temperament which has been exalted here, it would be kindness. It has always been the custom here on the Coast, when raising one's glass to say: "Here is kindness!" I have never heard the expression used elsewhere. And when Harrydick Ross, my nearest neighbor, says "Kindness!" it means just that.

Lone Cypress

ENRY MILLER'S PARADISE on the south coast soon felt the impact of civilization, as his Big Sur writing finally reached the pressrooms of America. Gradually, in the postwar fifties, his elysian outpost began to echo with the cacophony of tourism. By the end of the decade, a younger generation of artists and writers, dropout proto-beatniks, and other self-styled seekers of the truth descended on the beaches and valleys of the Pacific slope. Persistent journalists haunted the still sparsely populated artists' and writers' community in search of what some enterprising newcomer termed a "free love cult" reputed to be flowering somewhere in the redwood canyons.

Another manifestation of the human condition, the search for higher consciousness, led to Slate's Hot Springs below Partington Ridge. Henry Miller had left the Big Sur community to write out his days along another, more temperate California seacoast, and his friend, the great nature poet Eric Barker, had died in this country that he loved. The 1960s, a time of revolutionary fervor and violence, gave birth to a place called Esalen, once called Tok-i-toc, the sacred place of the Esselen tribelet.

A new vision of the human potential gathered momentum at the group therapy sessions at Esalen Institute, founded by Michael Murphy of Salinas, and under the influence of the distinguished Gestalt psychologist Fritz Perls. Men and women conceptualized a more enlightened future community, believing that the true message of the coast lies not in words or images but in the naked act of self-discovery before nature. Esalen became a mecca for thousands seeking inner awareness.

Also in the sixties, a wave of young pilgrims, many of them fugitives from the hippie communes of San Francisco's Haight-Ashbury or New York's East Village, swarmed the mountainsides of the Lucias or squatted under ancient redwoods in canyons away from the summer fog.

With the influx of people, the land seemed threatened with despoilation. The tough-spirited people of Big Sur responded to the challenges of overpopulation and the threat to the environment with stringent laws. But laws against hitchhikers, hippie-pilgrims, and tourists could not keep the seekers from their dream of paradise on the south coast.

Private real estate entrepreneurs and hotel developers extended the Monterey Peninsula resort community into the Big Sur wilderness. Excess profits from an inflating economy, fueled by the Vietnam War, were reinvested on the coast, bringing dropout businessmen and professional people, who gradually rehabilitated the old redwood cabins north of Lucia. And as the cabins were transformed with modern plumbing and electricity, new and more conventional homes appeared along Highway 1 to Carmel Highlands, until the land began to exhibit the sores and blemishes that were the end-product of uninspired designer-builders and pedestrian architects. Occasionally, a more refined, less ego-bound structure would appear in the camouflage of natural rock and gnarled trees. But this was the exception, a moment of oneness between man and nature that eventually became lost in the haphazard grid of coastal planning.

By the early 1970s, the horror of subdivision, which blights Santa Cruz and Half Moon Bay to the north, threatened to subvert the wise planning of the founding fathers and mothers, who had refused to let Big Sur become a coastal ghetto.

The menace of overdevelopment on the south coast was finally averted by the establishment of the California Coastal Commission Act of 1976, whose charter preserved coastal wilderness and beaches in the public interest. Private ownership of the shoreline was to give way to the concepts of sharing and conservation.

The unfortunate aftermath of state intervention during the late 1970s and early 1980s was a bitter, ongoing battle among local environmentalists, including the world-famous photographer, Ansel Adams, who had moved his studio to Carmel Highlands, and residential builders, realtors, and visionary designers, who argued for either stronger federal control or for the return of coastal jurisdiction to Monterey County. Responsible growth with ecological balance often became obstructed by a permit process that created a new kind of bureaucratic fascism, leaving, at the end of the legal trail, an uneasy compromise that returns a highly restricted plan for coastal development to the jurisdiction of Monterey County.

During recent times, this new plan has heralded a slow-down of growth throughout the county. In Carmel, the famous old Mission Ranch resort property was rescued from potential condo-development by actor, filmmaker, and former mayor, Clint Eastwood.

Today, still another subculture lurks in the mountains beyond Notley's Landing. Young rednecks, eccentric artists, self-styled mountain men, and, occasionally, marijuana growers camouflage themselves deep in Los Padres National Forest. Mountain men fight over water rights, while other fugitives disappear into the wilderness to band together like the cannibal-drummers in a Jean Luc Goddard film.

The peaceful anarchy of old California has given way to an uneasy truce between modern life-styles. In the sky over Big Sur, federal narcotics agents, flying helicopters developed in Vietnam, protect the wealthy, senior-citizen resort community that inhabits Carmel and Pebble Beach from real and imagined infiltration by the rebels in the mountains.

Yet throughout all the petty bickering, the silent presence of the coast, the essence of the land, remains timeless, aloof from the more transitory concerns of human avarice. For thus it has always been on the coast, in spite of the constant grinding and digging, and building and fighting, and buying and selling that has desecrated too much of the land from Monterey south past Point Lobos.

I lose faith in words in this country.
Better to leave unsaid
The poems which cannot describe the highest arcs
Of turning and turning hawks, the mountainous
Voyaging leisure of animal-changing clouds.
What words released from this granite shoulder
Can return like cliff-falling gull
Translating the mood of the sea.

— Eric Barker

THE IDYLLIC PATHWAY to the beach that George Sterling and his band of fellow artists merrily trod no longer echoes with the choruses of the "Abalone Song." The main thoroughfare of Carmel-by-the-Sea is now lined with expensive dress shops, Tudoresque teahouses, restaurants, real estate offices, antique and gift stores, and commercial art galleries. Little remains along the cleanly scrubbed sidewalks to suggest earlier days of bohemian abandon or colorful artistic individuality. The rocky inlets of Carmel Point that once held the campfires of Mary Austin and Jack London now give shelter to surfers and wet-suited scuba divers, who look curiously alien against the soft, white sand.

The area once renowned for its artists has become a wealthy resort community, whose galleries, with few exceptions, display commercial seascape painting, decorative modernism, and conservative portraiture that seldom approach the standards of the venerable National Academy of Design. As a result, the spirit of the creative avant-garde exists today not because of the Monterey Peninsula's artistic community but in spite of it. A few serious artists surface occasionally in such out-of-the-way places as Pacific Grove. And world-renowned musicians still perform at the esteemed Carmel Bach Festival. In *Travels with Charley*, John Steinbeck remarked that if Carmel's artist-founders returned to the peninsula, "they could not afford to live there, but it wouldn't go that far. They would instantly be picked up as suspicious characters and deported over the city line."

If art and architecture indeed reflect the spirit of past civilizations, what will the Monterey Coast reveal to a future generation? Fortunately, the understated simplicity of the later adobe residences of the Sánchez and Alvarado families has been preserved and restored by Californians who have become responsible custodians of the land. Preservation of the land has always been a concern of this enlightened minority — the founding ranchers of the south coast and the environmentalists of Monterey County — who form a firm line of resistance against the entrenched, agressive, building-trades industry and the real estate establishment.

All building cannot cease, but what comes next must respect the delicate ecological balance of the coast. Otherwise, the environment will become a threat to human wellness, and breakthroughs in medical science will be neutralized. If human beings are to remain civilized, individuals must become profoundly involved with the natural forms and spaces that nurture and shelter them. Humane architecture and clean energy systems will not desecrate the land. Nowhere is this vision more clearly evident than in the early organic adobe buildings of the Californians.

It is fitting that the descendants of Spanish California keep the gentle traditions of old Monterey alive. In the presence of Anita Abby Church, a restoration activist and a Native Daughter of California, whose life has been devoted to good works and whose grandmother was a doña in early California, one feels the generosity and hospitality of an earlier time. Each year in Monterey, guitars and castanets still echo in the old adobe courtyard of the Garden of Memories as the Merienda celebration relives the festivities of old California. Once more, families dance the fandango and the jota, and the Californians choose a señorita to preside over the day.

The serenity of dolce far niente still remains at the Carmel Mission and in the old adobes that have been lovingly restored by the conservationists of California. These structures recall a people who once lived close to the land and built their homes from its earth. They knew how to build heat-efficient, thick adobe walls that withstood the temblors of earthquake country. The simplicity and generosity of this life has been lost to the resort architecture and the ersatz Tudor buildings that crowd the Monterey Peninsula. Only recently has the concern for energy conservation and self-sufficiency revived the heritage of old California.

The austere natural beauty of the coast — cherished by generations of Californians — remains, in some places, as the early settlers found it. Thankfully, the shoreline from Point Lobos past Big Sur is being preserved. And a more profound understanding of human interaction with nature has created a new awareness, a holism that encompasses the coastal tradition.

In the quietude of an early morning on the coast, a person can be at one with the mysteries of the universe. In the words of Henry Miller:

> *Most everyone has known* one *moment in his life when he felt so good, so thoroughly attuned, that he has been on the point of exclaiming: "Ah, now is the time to die!" What is it that lurks here in the very heart of euphoria? The thought that it will not, cannot last? The sense of an ultimate? Perhaps. But I think there is another, deeper aspect to it. I think that in such moments we are trying to tell ourselves what we have long known but ever refuse to accept — that living and dying are one, that all is one, and that it makes no difference whether we live a day or a thousand years.*

The Spanish-speaking people of old California knew well the meaning of communion, of beauty in a ruin, the smell of adobe. Unlike their forefathers, they did not lust for gold nor dream of Empire. Perhaps the early Californians were the last honorable people on the land. But it is also true, as Henry Miller points out, that others have inherited the traditions of kindness and hospitality that define the higher quest for spirituality and humanity.

The great master artists and writers, the first settlers, and the environmental philosophers have sensed the essence of the coast — that moment of austere perfection when the human being is one with nature. A continuity appears, as Jeffers teaches us, in that same elemental force of light and sea that obsessed the poets of ancient Greece. Perhaps the Strait of Anián exists after all — in the northwest passage of the mind.

Down the coast the light is still holy. And the pale gold formations of the Pacific slope stand timeless against the water's edge. What remains is the great mirror of the sea, asking the best and the worst from us. It waits in light-struck, fog-bound silence to make music of the soul — to show the way to paradise.

The Author

FREDRIC HOBBS, multimedia artist and filmmaker, was born in Philadelphia and is a graduate of the Menlo School and Cornell University. After serving as an Air Force officer in air rescue, Hobbs maintained a studio in Madrid, Spain, where he attended the Academia de San Fernando de Belles Artes. In recent years, his studio has been located in the San Francisco Bay Area and on the Monterey Coast.

The artist has held 24 one–man exhibitions in galleries and museums, including the Museum of Science and Industry, Los Angeles, the San Francisco Museum of Modern Art, the California Palace of the Legion of Honor, and the Sierra Nevada Museum of Art, and has participated in traveling exhibitions of American art. His work is represented in such important permanent collections as the Museum of Modern Art and the Metropolitan Museum, New York, the San Francisco Museum of Modern Art, the Fine Arts Museums of San Francisco, and the Oakland Museum of Art and numerous others.

In the 1970s Fredric Hobbs pioneered a new, Post-Modernist artform known as ART ECO, which combined environmental technology, energy-producing sculpture, radical architecture, and New Medicine with self-sufficient life-style.

Hobbs has written, directed, and produced four feature motion pictures and a series for television. Currently, he is at work on an interactive–participatory television project entitled "FUTURENOW." Hobbs is the author of three books that include original drawings and he is listed in *Who's Who in America*.

Design and Typography

Gerald W. Stratford, is a fourth-generation Californian whose family has contributed to the Bay Area tradition of fine typography, printing, and bookbinding since 1906. Stratford currently heads Stratford Design Associates, a marketing group specializing in corporate identity and trademark development. While providing elegant design solutions to the corporate community, the firm designs books for the sheer joy of their production, and has produced volumes for the California Palace of the Legion of Honor and the DeYoung Museum as well as the award-winning *Private Collection* cookbook series.

The type for *Spirit of the Monterey Coast* was composed in complete pages on a Compaq Deskpro–286 computer, using MagnaType Software.

The typeface is Palatino, although we have adjusted its proportion by condensing the text type throughout the book so it maintains a letter height consistent with eleven-point with a letter width commensurate with ten-point. The result of this change in proportion is improved justification, despite the relatively short line length.

Originally designed by Herman Zapf in 1950, Palatino is reminiscent of the Venetian types of the fifteenth century but follows the influence of William Morris' Golden Type in its relatively even stroke width. The formation of letters in the earliest of Roman typefaces duplicated the look of hand lettering forms, and continued to do so well into the eighteenth century. Originally, calligraphers held their pens at an angle to the paper, and in the drawing of a rounded letter the broad nib produced the two areas of thickest stroke in diagonal opposition. Palatino has retained this characteristic, even though much of the type designed after 1700 emulated the more modern writing masters, who held their pens at right angles to the paper.

Acknowledgements

The publisher wishes to thank Deborah Johansen for her research and collaborative writing on Native Americans, Junípero Serra, the George Sterling – Mary Austin relationship, and A Land for Sale. Deborah Johansen is a free–lance writer living in Carmel Valley.

In addition we gratefully express our appreciation to the following people who generously helped with our research and production:

Alan Baldridge, *C.B. Von Niel Library, Hopkins Marine Station;*
Martha Bentley, *director, Mayo Mayes O'Donnell Library;*
Barbara Bennigson, *Editor;*
Margot Oliver Berkquist, *daughter of photographer, Myron Oliver;*
Ronald Bostwick, *Monterey author;*
Charlyn Hermes Brown, *Hermes Design;*
Anita Abby Church, *Native Daughters of California;*
Steve Crouch, *photographer;*
Sir Harry Downie, *curator, Mission San Carlos Borromeo;*
Betsy Finch, *Mayo Hayes O'Donnell Library;*
Pat Hathaway, *photo–archivist;*
Richard Gordon Henderson, *art collector*
Cisse Dore Hill, *author*
Rev. David Hill, *All Saints Church, Carmel;*
Carol Jones, *Monterey County Library;*
Col. Richard McFarland, *curator, Monterey Maritime Museum;*
Karen Nilsson, *Tioga Publishing Co.;*
Harrie Page, *Native Daughters of California;*
Linda Plummer, *John Steinbeck Collection, Salinas Public Library;*
Peg Richter, *Harrison Memorial Library;*
Geza St. Galy, *Carmel artist and ceramicist;*
Kendall L. Stratford, *history teacher, Sequoia School District*

This book is about the "spirit" of the Monterey Coast. It is not intended as a definitive history of the region. To those who wish to know more about the people and events described in this work the author recommends the following excellent sources:

Bennett, Melba Berry. *The Stone Mason of Tor House; the life and work of Robinson Jeffers.* W. Ritchie Press, Los Angeles, 1966.

Bostick, Daisy. *Carmel — At Work and Play.* 1925

Brower, David, ed. *Not Man Apart, lines from Robinson Jeffers.* Sierra Club, 1965.

Fink Augusta. *Monterey The Presence of the Past.* Chronicle Books, San Francisco, 1972.

Jeffers, Robinson. *Roan Stallion, Tamar and Other Poems.* The Modern Library, New York, 1935.

Lydon, Sandy. *Chinese Gold: the Chinese in the Monterey Bay Region.* Capitola Book Co., Capitola, California, 1985.

Mathes, W. Michael. *Vizcaino and Spanish Expansion in the Pacific Ocean, 1580 - 1630.* California Historical Society, San Francisco, 1968.

Margolin, Malcolm. *The Ohlone Way: Indian Life in the San Francisco – Monterey Bay Area.* Heyday Books, Berkeley, 1978.

Walker, Franklin. *The Seacoast of Bohemia.* Peregrine Smith Inc., Salt Lake City, 1973.

Index

Other Tioga Books You Will Enjoy

San Francisco Bay Area
LANDMARKS
Reflections of Four Centuries

Charles Kennard
Foreword by James D. Houston
author of *Californians*

"A lovely and unusual photographic history."
—The Pacific Sun

Handsome duotone photographs and historic quotations bring alive stories of the land and people around the Golden Gate. The author/photographer, British-born and architect-trained, presents the beauty of the natural scene and the architectural "marks" on the land. He photographed the same vistas recorded by early explorers, travelers, pioneers, and modern commentators.

Photographs. Index. Bibliography. 160 pages. Hardcover $19.95

PASSING FARMS: ENDURING VALUES
California's Santa Clara Valley

Yvonne Jacobson
"Local history is the best history."
—From the Foreword by Wallace Stegner

This handsome volume filled with old photogbraphs brings vividly alive the memory of California's Santa Clara Valley as the "Valley of Heart's Delight," a colorful bloom of orchards. Jacobson chronicles the dedication of her family and friends to farming, a way of life now vanishing across our country.

Photographs. 16 full-color plates. Index. 250 pages. Hardcover $29.95

CALIFORNIA'S SPANISH PLACE NAMES
What They Mean and How They Got There

Barbara and Rudy Marinacci
"Not simply a compilation of meanings, but a history and travel companion as well."
—Bay Views Magazine

Learn about California's rich heritage of Spanish names and the stories behind them. A handy travel guide, this resource book is infused with a sense of the land before the Spanish began "to name and claim" two centuries ago. Dictionary includes pronunciation and definitions of common Spanish words.

Drawings. Index. 267 pages. Softcover $9.95

CALIFORNIA CURRENTS
An Exploration of the
Ocean's Pleasures, Mysteries, and Dilemmas

Marie De Santis
Chemist and former
commercial fisherwoman

Are you aware that 85% of California's population lives within 35 miles of the ocean? This volume of personal essays will expand your understanding of the Pacific Ocean, from the mystery of the disappearing kelp to public policy. By a scientific storyteller, the book is a collage of her own experience — interviews, sea stories, natural history and politics. For people fascinated by the sea.

Drawings. Index. Marine Directory. 238 pages. Hardcover $15.95